THROUGH THESE EYES

MY MINISTRY TO THE MENTALLY ILL

Chaplain O.D. Thomas in front of the Main Building of Bryce Hospital.

THROUGH THESE EYES

MY MINISTRY TO THE MENTALLY ILL

BY OTIS DANIEL THOMAS

The Best of Times
Pelham, Alabama

ISBN:1-886049-06-8

Text and Cover design by Leslie Cummins
Cover photographs by Larry Thomas

Published by The Best of Times
147 Corporate Way
Pelham, Alabama 35214

Distributed by Southern Publishers Group
1-800-628-0903

To

CLYTIE MAE WOMACK THOMAS

my dear wife for 65 years

She was great in spiritual stature, a constant support, an invaluable companion. Her strength of character, brilliance of mind, and steadfast devotion made her as wonderful a partner as any man could want.

Dorothea Dix came to Alabama as early as 1849 to advocate the founding of a hospital for the mentally ill. This marker was erected by the Alabama Historical Commission 100 years later.

PROLOGUE

It was my privilege to work as chaplain with my spiritual brothers and sisters, some of Alabama's mentally ill, for 14 years. I entered intimately into their lives and problems and gained great respect, love and compassion for them.

This book is based upon many of my personal experiences with the mentally ill in a state mental hospital situation. Except for Dr. Sidney Tarwater, Dr. Adolph L. Blakeney, the Rev. B.W. Allen, my wife, and me, I have used fictitious names for all persons in order to maintain their privacy and save them from possible embarrassment. These are real human beings, not abstract personalities. But there is nothing at all fictitious about the events. I have been able to record patients' unspoken thoughts and unobserved experiences because they have told me about them at later dates.

My purpose in writing this book was to help those who read it to develop a deeper appreciation for the mentally ill and to plead for the public to respond to their needs. I also believe the public should have a better understanding of mental hospitals and the chaplain's place in them. Some parts of this book may seem harsh, but are not so intended. I have simply reported events as I observed them.

This book is written from the chaplain's viewpoint, not that of the psychiatrist. A chaplain's role is spiritual ministry to the patient, not medical treatment. The views expressed herein are not to be thought of as a substitute for psychiatry, nor do I mean to imply that one who is sick physically or mentally should dispense with medical care. Psychiatry deals with man in relation to himself and others. As chaplain I considered man's relationship with God and with others. These perspectives are often confused, but they are different.

Perhaps no one ever had more of a medieval idea of mental hospitals than I did when I began my work as chaplain. Having found myself in this work after 23 years in the ministry as a local church pastor, I asked myself, Why am I here among these people? Finally the answer came: To bring the love of God to them. In and of my own self I was unable to love them, but soon I began to feel God's love for these persons. I realized if I did not love the people I served, my efforts would be in vain and my ministry would count for little.

Some ministers looked upon the work of a mental hospital chaplain with pity and said to me, "You are just wasting time working with those people." Some asked, "Isn't your work awfully depressing?" To these I unhesitatingly replied, "I have never been happier in my life." Yes, happier than I ever was in the regular pastorate where I served for more than two decades. At the hospital I addressed hundreds of people every Sunday. I never had a more attentive and appreciative congregation.

My work was always interesting and full of opportunities for spiritual growth and for service to God through service to humanity. It was very satisfying and rewarding, maybe not in a material way, but in rewards that have eternal value. Surely, I did not want to be pitied in the least. Furthermore, I did not find nearly as many "pastoral headaches" serving the mentally ill as I did in my earlier ministry, although my former congregations were wonderful and appreciative.

People speak of the sacrifice I made in working among the

mentally ill. Is it a sacrifice to serve our Father in the only way he can be served—through service to our spiritual brothers and sisters? It is emphatically no sacrifice. Say rather it is a privilege. In my work I found peace and satisfaction beyond measure. I was indeed blessed and my reward was the love and appreciation in the hearts of the patients at the hospital. The love they expressed was overwhelming and made me feel humble indeed.

Healthy minds and bodies come with awareness of our God and his loving kindness and healing power. I saw many bodies rebuilt, minds improved or restored, faith regained, and lives renewed among those who had been hospitalized for years. As they left the hospital for home, many patients said, "I know I can face life better than when I came here. I am now stronger in body, mind and spirit." Many others wrote back to me to express similar words of gratitude.

Perhaps the stigma of mental illness is harder to bear than all other human afflictions and suffering. I would urge those who have loved ones in the sorrow and suffering of mental illness not to let their own faith fail them, and to rise above their despair through greater awareness of God's available help. The families and their loved ones who are going through mental suffering can give thanks that God is in control; that the healing power of love is being manifested; and that effective treatment of mental illness continues to improve.

OTIS DANIEL THOMAS
May, 1995

PROLOGUE

- 1 -

The early morning air in Tuscaloosa was crisp, and a gentle breeze swayed the boughs of the trees as the sun sprayed the landscape with autumn light. To the casual observer this day was dawning just like any other. Scanning the horizon through my windshield, I turned my car off the main city thoroughfare and drove down the long lane to Bryce Hospital. I passed between rows of sycamore and pine trees and through an iron gate. Once inside I saw huge oak trees on either side, friendly and wide-limbed, forming an arch overhead as I drew near the administration building, an imposing structure with a high, white central dome. There was an atmosphere of comfort all around.

The trees, grounds and three-story buildings resembled a college campus, perhaps even an extension of the neighboring University of Alabama. But as I got closer, I saw the iron bars on the windows and remembered that this was a very different kind of institution. The gently rolling lawns, the spreading trees and singing birds made everything appear calm, peaceful, serene.

These signs were misleading.

I would soon learn just how much human suffering, sorrow,

and despair were hidden behind those cloistered walls, those locked doors and barred windows. I didn't know that inside those buildings were all sorts of needy people with troubled minds and fearful souls.

Trouble brought me to Bryce. This day, October 5, 1951, marked the beginning of my job as the first chaplain at The Alabama Mental Hospital, commonly called Bryce after its first superintendent.

Only a year before, I had been happy and secure as a pastor serving a local Methodist (now United Methodist) congregation. During my three years there I had visited every family in the community; Sunday school attendance had more than doubled; night services were well attended; church finances were in good shape; and many inactive younger members had begun attending regularly. I thought all was well with the congregation and my life.

One Sunday morning I referred to Adolph Hitler, stressing Jesus's command to love our enemies and pray for those who despitefully use us. Some members of the congregation strongly disagreed with me. They had lost loved ones in World War II and still had deep emotional wounds from the war. That evening the church board met and I was not invited. Although this was unusual, I didn't give it serious thought at the time. Later, I realized that that meeting probably was the turning point in my standing with the congregation.

It's also possible that my graduate studies were causing tensions of which I was unaware. Before the incident occurred I had enrolled at The University of Alabama to work toward a master's degree in sociology. Years before, I had attended Birmingham Southern College, then obtained bachelor of arts and bachelor of divinity degrees from Southern Methodist University. I didn't ask approval from the church's official board about continuing my education because it seemed unnecessary. In retrospect, this was a mistake.

Social reformer Dorothea Dix persuaded the Alabama Legislature to establish The Alabama Insane Hospital in 1852.

The hospital was named for Dr. Peter Bryce, who served as superindendent for 22 years after its founding.

Soon after the sermon mentioning Hitler, the annual Methodist conference met, during which appointments would be made for the next year. It was customary for ministers to be informed of any changes in their appointments before assignments were announced on the last day of the conference. I fully expected to be reappointed to the church I was serving.

I heard my name called and learned that I was expected to relocate to a church 150 miles away. I was flabbergasted and dismayed. Not only was I working toward a degree at the university, but my oldest son was a student there and my wife and I had plans for our two younger boys to be educated there also. To go so far away would have disrupted all of our lives.

When I joined the North Alabama Conference of the Methodist Church in the early 1920's, I promised to go wherever the conference sent me. This time, however, I felt it was asking too much of me and my family and that it was unfair. My wife, Clytie Mae, and I talked it over, prayed about it, and then I called the presiding elder (now called district superintendent) for my district. I should have made my family's need to remain near the university known to him earlier, but had not recognized the need to do so. He said he couldn't do anything for me and I would have to call the bishop. I spoke with the bishop, who told me he couldn't help me other than to give me a leave of absence to go to college.

So my family and I were faced with moving out of the parsonage in less than three days because the next pastor was on his way. Clytie Mae and I had been in this ministry since our marriage in 1928. We had been moving from place to place and church to church for more than 20 years. We owned little other than our clothing because all parsonage furnishings, even dishes and silverware, belonged to each church.

We searched for a house to rent and found an unfurnished one near the campus. One of our former church members and his wife brought us a used refrigerator that was in good condition. I made a table out of lemon crates and Clytie Mae improvised the rest. I don't remember what we did for beds or cookware or anything else. This crisis was very painful for me and my family and I don't remember much about how we managed. I had no income and my family was depending on me.

Slowly, things began to change for the better. One of my professors asked me to teach his Saturday class, for which he paid me $75 a month. The presiding elder asked me to fill an unexpected pastoral vacancy at a small local church at a salary of $90 a month. Clytie Mae got a job working with senior citizens and one of the boys took a paper route. All these things helped relieve the pressure.

Within a year I earned my master's degree in sociology. Clytie Mae and I had discussed our situation and concluded that teaching would provide a more stable life for our family than a pastorate. Shortly before graduation I sent out 20 resumes with cover letters seeking a college-level teaching position. I got no positive response. There were no openings; at this time enrollment was down because of the war in Korea. I was trying my best for my family, yet nothing seemed to be working. I didn't know what more I could do. I was at the end of my rope.

One evening as I left the university library, I was over-whelmed by hopelessness and despair. My family's future weighed heavily on me: I needed to pray. I didn't want to be seen by passersby, so I moved close to the building, behind the shrubbery. I got down on my knees, but that wasn't enough. I bowed down until my forehead rested on the ground. "God," I whispered, "I've gone as far as I can by myself. I need your help. I thought you wanted me to preach, but that didn't work out. Then I thought teaching was the answer, but there's no place for me. I can't think of anything else to do. You've got to help me: no one else can. Just point me in the right direction and I'll go anywhere and do anything you say. Thy will be done."

I lifted my head from the ground and rose to my feet. I felt lighter, as if an actual weight had gone from my shoulders. I walked home, no longer worrying, and knowing that somehow there would be a change.

A few days later my wife returned from a Methodist women's meeting and asked me if I would like to work at the state mental hospital. Some of the members had told Clytie Mae that the hospital was going to hire its first chaplain. I said that I'd be interested; at least it would relieve the financial pressure on my family. Within days I received copies of two letters writ-ten by prominent local businessmen to the hospital superinten-dent, Dr. Sidney Tarwater, recommending me for the job as chap-lain. Encouraged, I called Dr. Tarwater and made an appoint-ment for an interview. At his office we talked briefly and he offered me the position at a salary of $375 a month. That night at our supper table we had a lot to be thankful for and happy about. Our family had more security that night than we had had in almost a year.

I walked with a steady gait toward the main building. I was 53 years old with a sprinkle of gray in my hair, which I wore combed straight back. I stood five feet eight inches tall and weighed 150 pounds. As I drew near the old domed building, I had an uncomfortable feeling. What will my friends in the ministry and others say when they learn I am chaplain at a mental hospital? I thought, What if I can't do the job? Well, if I can't take it, I can go back into the pastorate, but I certainly will tackle it. Soon I'll know what it is like here.

My only previous contacts with a mental hospital were when I visited a friend here several years ago for just a few minutes and, later, at my job interview. After accepting the post as chaplain, I read a book entitled *Out of Sight, Out of Mind*. This was a report based on the experiences of many conscientious objectors who chose to work in mental institutions rather than go to war. It spoke of filth and vermin, bleak and barren walls, sorry food, overcrowded conditions, inadequate staff, untrained personnel, and mistreatment of patients, all to be found in mental hospitals. It made such a profoundly negative impression on me that I almost recoiled from entering the chaplaincy. I had also seen a highly publicized Hollywood movie, *The Snake Pit*, depicting the horrors of a mental institution. With this limited background I was soon to learn firsthand about life and conditions as they actually were behind the hospital's locked doors and barred windows. I felt very unprepared.

In spite of a feeling of uncertainty as to what was before me, I felt that somehow I had been called for this new field of service. That was the only way I could explain my presence here. Inside the building, I thought to myself, Well, here I am and here it is. Is this a "snake pit" like I read about in the book and saw in the movie? Is it a prison I am going into, or is it really a hospital for those who are mentally ill? Just exactly what is it?

I reported immediately to the superintendent's office. As I opened the door, Dr. Tarwater smiled and said in a soft, pleasant manner, "Good morning, chaplain. We are glad to have you with us. Come in and sit down."

The superintendent was a quiet, unassuming man. He had

Dr. James Sidney Tarwater was hospital super-indendent from 1950 to 1970.

been a doctor at the hospital for 25 years before being appointed superintendent. His responsibility for nearly 5,000 mentally ill patients and nearly 1,000 employees weighed heavily upon him. He knew many of those confined to the hospital blamed him for keeping them there and not letting them return to their homes, but he accepted their criticism.

He knew many of the employees were unhappy with their low wages. He was unable to hire enough trained people and the wards were overcrowded. As superintendent he had many decisions to make every day, yet in all of these he tried to look at every side of the subject before coming to a conclusion.

THROUGH THESE EYES

Restricted by an inadequate budget, Dr. Tarwater frequently spoke to community groups to acquaint them with the needs of the hospital. He was constantly seeking more money from the state legislature to improve facilities, personnel, and training programs. He would often say, "There is nothing wrong with our hospital that money won't cure."

Dr. Tarwater remarked to me, "As you go about your work, you will want to keep in mind that this is a *mental* hospital, a hospital for people with sick minds and nervous disorders. We do not call it a lunatic hospital or an insane asylum, nor any of the other terms which are even less compassionate." I was glad to hear these words, for many times I had heard people poke fun at the hospital by calling it a nut house, a booby hatch, or a cuckoo house—references I had never been able to approve.

"I'm sure, doctor," I remarked, "that you will be very helpful in helping me find my place and my work here. I know I'll be depending on you, especially at first, when I'm just getting acquainted."

Dr. Tarwater replied, "Since you are our first chaplain in the 90-year history of the hospital, yours will be a pioneer work here. I shall be glad to help in any way I can." Looking at his watch, he added, "Our staff meets every morning at eight. Suppose we go there now."

At the staff meeting, Dr. Tarwater presided at the head of a long table with the doctors, head nurse, dentist and chaplain seated along the sides. Shortly after the hospital's eight o'clock whistle blew, he turned and called each member of the staff by name to see if he or she had any report since the previous meeting.

"Nothing to report," said Mrs. Josephine Hutchens, the director of nursing.

"Nothing," said Dr. Mitchell Rolf.

"Nothing," echoed Dr. George Sterling.

Dr. John Morgan reported. "Henry Fowler died yesterday after a shock treatment. It must have been caused by a weak heart. He was a small man, 74 years old. He asked for the shock treatments, which had seemed to help him when he was here previously.

"A few days ago Mr. Fowler was found with a belt around his neck, looking for a place to tie it. It appeared he was planning to commit suicide. We gave him another shock treatment, thinking it would help him. We contacted the family by phone and the undertakers have removed his body."

"One of our ladies attempted suicide," reported another doctor. "I was called at 2:30 this morning. She had nicked her neck with a broken razor blade. She said she found it in the parking lot. She had told some of the ladies on her ward that she was considering suicide. We were able to quiet her down," he said.

"I had a death," said another. "Jack Kimbrell was found dead in his bed this morning by the ward attendant. I could find no marks on him. He was 90 years old and had been here as a patient 60 years. It seemed to be quite natural. He has no people that we can locate. He will have to be buried here."

Dr. Morgan spoke again. "We had two men escape last evening. After supper, they hid on the back porch behind some sacks of vegetables. After everyone had left the kitchen, they broke out the screen wire and got away in the dark. The police department, the highway patrol and their families have been notified."

Dr. Milton Rivers, who had responsibility for all surgical cases in addition to responsibility for the Ladies' Receiving Building, reported, "I've had four hip operations in the last week and have one more to do."

Dr. Tarwater remarked, "It concerns me that we have so many of our people getting hurt. What is the reason? Are we somehow to blame?"

Dr. Rivers elaborated, "One was getting a bath and dropped the soap. As she was trying to get it, she stepped on the soap and slipped down. One was in the dining room and stepped on some food that had spilled on the floor and fell. An elderly man who is rather tottery was standing in a doorway. Another man wanted him to get out of his way and gave him a push. He fell. One patient wet on the floor; another stepped in it and slipped. As one man was chasing another out of his room, he slipped and fell on the floor. We've been having more than our usual share of falls lately." After a moment's pause, Dr. Rivers continued, "The bones of these old folks are brittle like chalk and break easily."

Dr. Tarwater said, "I wish something could be done."

"So do I," replied Dr. Rivers. "It would save me a lot of work!"

Dr. Tarwater motioned toward me and remarked, "I would like now to present Chaplain Thomas, who is joining our hospital staff. He has just received a master's degree in sociology here at the university. His studies should prove helpful to him in his work with us."

After a brief pause, he continued, "Psychiatry has learned to make an accurate diagnosis and to recommend a useful plan, but psychiatry cannot furnish the motivation which will make the patient want to follow the plan. We believe our chaplain can help us here. In this spirit, we have invited him to join us." Then turning to me, he said, "We are glad to have you with us, chaplain. Suppose you go with Dr. Rivers today to get you oriented. He will see to it that you get acquainted with things."

After the staff meeting had adjourned, one of the doctors remarked as he walked down the hall with me, "I don't know how it is in your profession, but when a doctor comes to work in a mental hospital, he stoops mighty low. He stoops about as low as one can stoop."

I shook my head vehemently. "Doctor, I'm new here as you know, but I can't agree with you—not yet anyway. Pardon me for being so frank, but I believe you are wrong in your attitude. I see this as a great challenge and opportunity for a doctor and for a chaplain. I believe it is whatever we make it. I may come to agree with you, but not now."

The hospital's professional staff began its day's work with seven doctors, a superintendent and his assistant, one dentist, eight registered nurses, and now one chaplain to care for the physical, mental and spiritual needs of nearly 5,000 people. It was an inadequate force.

The duties of the doctors included visiting all the people on their assigned wards and meeting with relatives who had come to learn about the condition of a loved one. In addition, they had to answer many letters of inquiry from people who could not come in person and who waited for any word of encouragement from the doctor about the progress and possibility of recovery of their loved one. There were no psychologists or social workers. Some of the doctors were approaching retirement age in their practice of medicine and had come here to work. Each of them had responsibility for as many as 900 patients. The single dentist worked from dawn to dusk.

Although I had been at the hospital less than an hour, I had already found a serious-minded staff undertaking a herculean task. I thought of the entire staff as being there to represent the love of God in action and I was determined to bring this love to my charges.

Dr. Rivers, who had lingered in the staff room to speak further with Dr. Tarwater, stopped at the door of my office and said, "All right, chaplain. I'm ready to go. I believe you are to go with me today."

I nodded and said, "I'm ready."

This building, formerly for women's admissions, is now also used for men.

-2-

I was not present when some of the events in this chapter—and other events recorded elsewhere—occurred, but was told of them later by the persons involved.

Mrs. James Collin had just completed cooking breakfast and was eating with her husband and three small children when two deputy sheriffs knocked at the front door. She was startled; it was a bit early for visitors. Her husband went to answer the door. One of the deputies announced that he had papers authorizing him to take Mrs. Collin to the mental hospital.

"No, *no!*" she exclaimed in dismay. "There must be some mistake." Then turning to her husband and trying to remain calm, she asked inquiringly, "James, what does this mean?" In her eyes there was accusation.

He stood there, silent, with a smirk on his face. The smallest daughter ran to her mother and, throwing her arms around her parent's neck, turned to the uniformed officers and cried, "Don't take my mother away." The older children watched anxiously. Mrs. Collin shuddered and tears formed in her eyes.

Her husband broke into laughter and said, "Take her away!"

Without giving the woman time to dress, the deputies carried her away in her housecoat, even though the weather was chilly. She saw it was useless to resist and went meekly. On the way to the hospital she asked, "Why has James done this to me? I'm not crazy and there's nothing wrong with my mind." The officers were silent. They ignored her demands for an explanation.*

I had been standing near the receptionist's desk while Dr. Rivers took care of some phone calls and dictated a few letters before going on the wards. While I waited there, the front door opened and a slim, attractive young woman with auburn hair was ushered in by deputy sheriffs. She moved calmly but reluctantly toward the desk. Her red eyes testified that she had been weeping. One of the deputies presented the necessary com-

---

* During my time at Bryce (1951-1965) there were no clear standards for commitment. The vast majority of patients came to Bryce by way of a probate court commitment; petitions to courts were signed locally, and patients were frequently transported to the hospital by their county sheriff's department. The person may or may not have been seen by a doctor. Many people at Bryce *were* mentally ill and needed to be hospitalized, but because there were no safeguards against false charges, the process could be abused and some people were sent to Bryce unjustly. It was possible for anyone to have another person committed; they did not have to be related by blood or marriage.

It was not until a federal court decided the case of *Lynch* v. *Baxley* in 1972 that definite standards were set for commitment and the problem of abuse addressed.

Under the criteria for commitment established by the court, there must be proof that a person is mentally ill, a person must have committed a recent overt act which would establish mental illness, and a person must be a harm to himself or others. For its part, the state is required to make treatment available to patients, and that treatment must be in the least restrictive environment. Implicit in this last requirement is the state's responsibility to establish local mental health centers.

The *Lynch* v. *Baxley* decision further mandated that every patient's case *be reviewed annually* and a decision made whether to recommit or discharge that person. It became necessary to create transitional and group homes, foster homes, and halfway houses. Bryce had a large geriatric population and many of these patients were placed successfully in nursing homes in their home counties.

Bryce had had as many as 5,200 patients attended by a staff of

mitment papers, which stated, "Mrs. James (Edith) Collin is insane, and her own and the public welfare demand that she be sent to the hospital for insane persons for custody and treatment."

The lady at the desk read the papers to see if they were in order. Looking toward the woman and smiling pleasantly, she asked, "Are you Mrs. Edith Collin?" Mrs. Collin nodded that she was. Smiling again and trying to be as helpful as possible to alleviate fear, the receptionist said, "Mrs. Collin, you will have to take off your rings. We will keep them for you so they won't get lost. I'm sorry; this is a rule here." Mrs. Collin complied, slowly handing her rings to the receptionist. At this moment a

---

800 persons. In the 1990's there are approximately 1,200 patients and 2,000 employees. This greatly reduced patient/staff ratio resulted partly from the changes mandated by *Wyatt v. Stickney* (1970), which dealt with standards for mental health treatment facilities.

There are four types of commitments to state mental hospitals. The majority of patients are referred by doctors and mental health centers using the probate court commitment. A petition is signed at the county level and the patient taken to Bryce.

A second method is the circuit court commitment in which a person has been charged with a crime, which can be minor but is nearly always some felonious act. The legal authorities recommend that the person be sent to Bryce for testing and evaluation to determine whether he or she is mentally ill. These patients are usually housed in the unit for the criminally mentally ill. After the evaluation is made the results are considered by a lunacy commission which was created by law. This commission decides whether or not the patient knew the difference between right and wrong and is considered competent to stand trial.

A third method for commitment to Bryce is voluntary commitment, which is rarely used. Since the creation of the local health care system, patients who need acute care are usually treated at home or in the psychiatric ward of a local hospital. However, long-term care for those with chronic mental illness is found at Bryce.

The fourth method is the governor's commitment. In this case the person in question is in prison when he becomes mentally ill. At that point the governor authorizes that the prisoner be sent to Bryce. Treatment is given and, if the patient improves, he is discharged from the hospital and returned to prison.

ward attendant in a gray uniform appeared at the desk.

"Mrs. Collin, this is one of your ward attendants. She will take over from here and help you," said the receptionist pleasantly. "It is her job to give you every assistance."

After they entered the ward, the attendant locked the door behind them and said, "Take off your clothes, Mrs. Collin, so you can take a bath."

"Why should I take a bath?" Edith asked calmly. "I had a bath last night. What does all this mean? I don't need a bath."

When her bath was finished, Mrs. Collin was given state clothes. She asked, "Why can't I keep on my housecoat since my husband didn't send any clothes for me?"

"No one wears their own clothes on this ward, Mrs. Collin, except when they have visitors," explained the attendant. When Edith was dressed, the attendant said to her, "Now, let's go up where the other ladies are." She led her along the hall, introduced her to another attendant in a large sitting room with many other women, then showed her to a seat on a long wooden bench.

Mrs. Collin had asked her husband *why*; she had asked the deputies *why*; and she had asked the attendant *why* another bath. Now she appeared totally bewildered. As she sat there in a strange place, looking around her at strange faces and hearing strange noises, a terrible sense of loneliness came over her. Covering her face with her hands, she cried softly, her body trembling, "Oh, God, not this! Oh, God, *no!*"

Words from scripture came to her mind: Be still and know that I am God. . . . I will never leave you nor forsake you. . . . I will be with you always. Lifting her drooped body, she rubbed her eyes with the backs of her hands, saying softly, "Thank you, Father."

I had grown tired of standing, so I took a seat in the reception area, still waiting for the doctor to take me with him and introduce me to the ward attendants with whom I was to work.

As I sat there, a portly woman came in with her husband. She wore a tailored, burgundy dress, had brown hair and dark brown eyes, and gave the impression of being a woman of intelligence and refinement. She walked gracefully to the desk. Her husband presented commitment papers which gave her name as Mrs. Martha Richardson. The receptionist asked her to take off her rings and other jewelry.

Mrs. Richardson looked at the young woman in disbelief. "Why do you want me to take off my wedding rings?" she asked in astonishment. "I've never had them off since my husband put them on my fingers. They mean a great deal to me. Why must I take them off?"

"You will have to take them off, Mrs. Richardson," explained the receptionist firmly. "You might lose them while you are here."

Suddenly realization seemed to dawn on the woman. She turned quickly to her husband, her eyes flashing, her body stiffening; she spoke with a high-pitched voice. "What is this, a frame-up?"

Without saying a word, her husband showed her the commitment papers and she read, "Mrs. Martha Richardson is hereby committed to Alabama State Mental Hospital by reason of insanity." She shuttered violently and screamed.

"You didn't tell me I was being committed here," she exploded. "You told me I was coming for a checkup. I'm not crazy and you know it as well as I do." With that she snatched the papers of commitment and tore them into shreds, then shouted to her husband, "You are the one who needs to be here, if anybody does! You're the one that's loony."

He remained silent as the receptionist spoke calmly but firmly, "Give your rings to your husband, Mrs. Richardson."

With that, the woman took off her rings and flung them as far as she could, at the same time screaming at her husband, "Damn you!"

As he stooped to pick up the rings, the receptionist and an

attendant ushered Mrs. Richardson toward the hallway. She resisted but the two ladies pushed firmly against her back. When she had moved across the threshold, the door shut and the key turned in the lock. Mrs. Richardson had arrived.

After the routine bath and change to hospital clothes, accompanied by much protest from Mrs. Richardson and the usual explanation by the ward attendant, the patient joined the women in the sitting room. Here she would have her introduction to the other inmates.

Approximately 50 women were in this room, most of them sitting on long benches against the walls, or in an occasional rocking chair or straight chair. Or, one might be found lying on the floor or on a bench trying to sleep. Some were calm while others were agitated. A vase of flowers sat on a large table in the center of the living room, but the walls were bare.

A strange feeling came over Mrs. Richardson as she found a seat among the mentally disturbed women. She looked around apprehensively.

"These women are staring at me," she thought to herself. "They don't like me. I'm not welcome here."

Engrossed in thoughts of their own, most of them didn't notice her. Seeing a dog-eared magazine on the table, Mrs. Richardson picked it up and went to a chair in a far corner of the room away from the others. She would just do some reading. She sat down and began to turn the pages aimlessly, then, raising her head, looked about the room and studied the faces furtively.

"Why are all these women here?" she asked herself. "That young blonde with a pretty face and light hair that they call Sandra is probably a prostitute," she thought. "That rosy-cheeked fat woman, I wonder what her trouble is. She's probably a criminal. Then there's that thin girl with a silly laugh; she doesn't seem very bright. There is that old lady carrying a pot of flowers about balanced on her head. She must be real batty. What a bunch of loons they have put me in with."

Over at the table, Mrs. Richardson saw a woman writing a letter for another who sat in a wheelchair, crippled by arthritis in her hands, her knuckles and fingers twisted. Down the hallway a woman's voice was calling, "Nurse, nurse! I want a drink of water." The patient rattled the barred door of her room as she repeated, "Nurse, nurse! I want a drink of water." The cry was insistent and harsh.

Some of the women were sitting in silence, as if a hopeless death sentence had been pronounced upon them. One was thinking: They are going to kill me tonight. Some were placid; one read a magazine; some stared at nothing; another stood at the window and gazed silently outside. Two or three paced the floor aimlessly; one picked up scraps of paper, straws and such and placed them carefully in her pocket, oblivious to her surroundings. Some sat with bodies and heads bent, chins touching their chests; others muttered unintelligible words. Occasionally two or three would talk briefly. Some of these women were elderly, others were middle-aged or younger, and there were a few hardly out of their teens. They ran the gamut from pretty to very plain.

These were some of the scenes in the Ladies' Receiving Building (LRB).* My work began here. Every morning the nurse would turn the key in the door and enter the sitting room along with Dr. Rivers and a ward attendant. This was routine daily work for the doctor, as it would soon become for me. Occasionally Dr. Rivers would speak a "good morning!" to a patient. He

---

*When patients arrived at Bryce, they were admitted at either the Ladies' or Men's Receiving Building. These new patients were housed on the "disturbed" wards until they became oriented to their surroundings. As they became quieter, they were moved to general wards.

Patients with specific problems were gathered in particular wards, such as the tubercular ward, the criminal ward, or an "untidy" ward. The patients in this latter type of ward were unable to control their bodily functions.

might pause to ask one her name or just turn to the nurse and say, "What is her name?" If a nurse or attendant could not recall the patient's name, she would likely get a word of scolding from the doctor. He expected them to know the names of everyone on the ward. After all, that was part of their job.

Dr. Rivers, who had responsibility for 200 mentally ill women in the LRB and for all the hospital surgery, was a tall, dark and handsome bachelor. Some of the female patients openly claimed he was their husband. Others secretly entertained the idea. One might ask an employee, "How is my husband?" When asked, "Who?" she would reply, "Why, Dr. Rivers, of course," as if the other person were very forgetful.

One patient with ground privileges would sit on the lawn and watch the doctor as he went in and out of the building. A little old lady in one of the back wards would ask, "How is my baby doll?" She carried a pencil with her and would write lengthy love letters to him on toilet paper, wrap and tie them with a cloth string, and ask any one who would volunteer to take these notes to her "baby doll."

Not all the women were fans of Dr. Rivers, however. There were those who hated him because he gave them shock treatments* or refused to let them go home.

---

* Electroconvulsive therapy (ECT), or "shock treatment," as it is commonly called, was in use as a treatment for mental patients during my tenure at Bryce Hospital (1951-1965). The mechanism of the therapy is not fully understood.

At Bryce, therapy usually consisted of ten treatments given at the rate of three per week. On any given day, six or seven patients were scheduled for therapy.

The patient lay on a padded table in the ECT treatment room and was held down by three nurse's aids to help counteract the convulsions produced by the shock. A registered nurse placed electrodes at the temporal region of the skull and the doctor opened a circuit to pass an electrical charge through the patient's brain for a few milliseconds. The patient was then carried on a stretcher to a bed in a small ward nearby and monitored for the rest of the day.

Ignoring those who admired him and those who did not, Dr. Rivers went about his duties each day, working early and late to do what he could for the 200 women for whom he was responsible. With new women coming to the hospital constantly, he tried to have them ready to return home within three to six months. If he failed in this, he would transfer them over to the main building where about 2,200 other women were confined to their wards. Many of the women mistakenly thought that as long as they remained in the LRB they were there only for observation, but if

---

Because the shock would cause convulsions powerful enough to severely strain muscles and even break bones, the patient was given a drug just before the treatment to relax his muscles and thereby reduce the violence of the spasms. However, this medication relaxed involuntary as well as voluntary muscles, and there was a very brief period during which the person could not breathe. Immediately after the shock, oxygen was administered, but the patient had had the very unpleasant experience of not being able to breathe for a moment, and this was one of the factors which contributed to the considerable fear many persons had of shock treatment. Another cause of fear was the memory loss, apathy, bland facial expressions, and scrambled thoughts which often followed treatment and lasted for several hours.

There was no attempt to explain to the patients what would happen to them during shock therapy. The patients, however, discussed their experiences among themselves and the result was a general fear and dread of ECT. Some patients erroneously believed the treatments were used as a punishment for bad behavior. On the other hand, there were those who felt so much better after this therapy that they would request ECT when they felt their symptoms returning. Occasionally a patient would tell me that he or she was scheduled for shock treatment that day and ask me to pray for him or her.

Nowadays ECT is not used at Bryce, but when it is required, patients are referred to nearby DCH Regional Medical Center. A candidate for therapy must have a case review by an "extraordinary treatment" committee which asks if medication can possibly accomplish the same result. Electroconvulsive therapy is used as a last resort.

The procedure has changed, but is as effective as ever, and is less traumatic for the patient. Now there are milder experiences of memory loss and apathetic gazing into space, and the patient is able to walk about shortly after treatment.

transferred to the main building, or old building as it was called, then they thought they had been declared insane and were stuck there for the rest of their lives.

I sat waiting patiently by the reception desk. Dr. Rivers finally appeared and said, "Chaplain, I'm sorry to keep you waiting so long. I just had to dictate some letters and make some phone calls. I'll introduce you to the folks on the disturbed ward and leave you there. We had an attendant come to work today with liquor on her breath. We can't have that sort of thing. I had to get rid of her. That's something we don't stand for."

"Dr. Rivers, who is this man with you? Is he another doctor?" asked a lady who was standing near the door of the disturbed ward as we entered with the nurse and attendant. "I've never seen him before. Is he your new doctor?"

"No, he is a preacher," explained Rivers. "He has come to be our chaplain."

"What's his name?"

"This is Chaplain Thomas," he replied.

Turning to shake hands with me, the patient said, "I am Ethel Norwood. I'm glad you are here. We surely do need a chaplain or something. You will be good for our morale. Maybe we can get some of our faith back."

Several ladies drew near, some reaching out to shake hands with me, while others just stood and looked on apprehensively. A slender, young brunette came up and asked in a sharp voice, "Who are you?"

"I'm Chaplain Thomas; I've come to be your chaplain here."

"I wouldn't admit it if I were you," she said, "unless you are sincere." Continuing to look me over with a quizzical eye, she stated, "You must not be much of a preacher to come to work with us crazy folks here in this hell hole. What happened? Did they kick you out of your church?"

Some of the women standing near me looked at her, then looked toward me to see what I would say. I thought it prudent to keep silent but Mrs. Norwood, who had first greeted me as I came on the ward, said, "Shame on you, Sharon, to talk to our chaplain like that! He's here to give us some faith."

Quickly Sharon flung back at Mrs. Norwood, "You go to hell, you old bitch!" Then turning again, she spoke in a loud voice, "I don't want any damn preacher's pity. Furthermore, I don't like preachers. They're all crooks. You're a crook too," she said defiantly. "You're just like all the rest!"

I tried to remain calm and disregard her barbs, for I saw that she was agitated and I thought she might strike me. I was surprised to feel a certain fear of her. She gave me a hostile look and continued, "I want to get out of here and back to civilization. All these folks are goddamn idiots, and you are too!" With one final menacing look at me she turned and walked away briskly to an adjoining room, much to the relief of everyone. The doctor looked at me with an apologetic expression.

I remained silent as I watched Sharon leave. I tried not to think of her as a mental patient or a crazy person, but as a human being deeply hurt. I tried to look on her with compassion and as one who was going through a very difficult experience. The ward attendant who had been standing nearby during Sharon's tirade followed her and said in a low voice, "Sharon, you ought not talk that way about the chaplain. That is not going to help you any. He has come here to help us." Sharon was sullen and silent. She merely turned away to look into space.

Dr. Rivers moved on to other work while I remained to get better acquainted and talk with those who might seek my help. One young woman, after looking me over, turned to another patient sitting next to her and remarked, "The chaplain is real good looking."

In the 1950's and 1960's, many patients lived in bleak cubicles such as this.

The other agreed, "Yes, he is, but he's not exactly a Clark Gable." They got up and came over to speak to me.

"I'm Lynn," said the pretty, slender blonde.

"I'm Joleen," said the other. She had lovely auburn hair and blue eyes. Each extended a hand in greeting. I took both hands cordially and the girls smiled. "It must take a strong mind to work with these people," said Lynn. Then she asked, "Did you ever see the movie, *The Snake Pit*?"

"Yes, I did and I read the book, too," I said.

"This is it right here," Lynn replied. Then, changing the subject, she asked, "What shall I call you?"

"My official title is Chaplain Thomas."

"Chaplain! I don't like that," she said. Placing her hand to her head as if trying to decide, she added, "Preacher! I don't care for that either. Anyway, did you ever drink whiskey?"

To this I simply answered, "No, I've never tasted it." She looked at me in astonishment.

"Did you ever run with the women?"

"Just one," I replied, "my wife. We've been married for 24 years."

"You mean you never step out on your wife?" Lynn asked. "Come on, you can tell us!"

"That's true."

"You've missed a lot of fun in life," she observed.

"Maybe so," I replied, "but I've also had a lot of fun in life, so I guess that makes up for it."

"You're an unusual man," Lynn commented. "Most men do step out on their wives—even preachers do." Then she asked further, "Did you ever run around with other women before you were married?"

"Oh, yes, I dated several girls," I replied.

"You were shy, weren't you?" she said with a wink.

"You may call it that if you want to."

Joleen had been standing there with her arm around Lynn while listening to the dialogue. She spoke. "I want to ask you a question. You don't have to answer it if you don't want to." Lowering her voice almost to a whisper, she said, "The thing I wonder is, did I act like some of these folks on this ward when I first came here?" Her eyes made a swift glance toward the other women. She continued, "I watch what they do and I ask myself, 'Joleen, did you act like that?' Then I say, 'No, of course not.' But I still wonder. Maybe I did. Maybe I acted just like them and didn't know it at the time."

Sharon had rejoined the group and interrupted by saying impatiently, "I want to get out of here. I don't like those electric shock treatments. I haven't had a pill, a shot in the arm, or a shot in the butt since I've been here," she said, pointing respectively to her mouth, arm and hip as she spoke. "All I've had was those awful shock treatments. I hate them so much. I don't want any more."

When Sharon paused, Lynn asked me, "Are you allergic to women?"

"No," I replied, "not that I know of. I don't think I would be here if I were. Why do you ask?"

"I saw you rubbing your nose," she explained. They laughed together.

Lynn looked at my tie and remarked, "You have on a pretty tie. It matches your blue eyes. Blue eyes mean you're sincere. That's my belief, anyway." I thanked her. She added, "I bet you were almost handsome when you were young."

"I'm allergic to preachers," said Sharon with a sneer, as she walked away.

"I'm allergic to some things, too," I replied, glancing her way.

"What?" she asked sharply, turning to me defiantly.

"Sin," I replied.

"I'm not. I'm for it," was her belligerent statement.

A plump woman with rosy cheeks walked up, smiling. "Hey, let me whisper something to you." With her hand cupped around her mouth, she whispered, "I'll give you my virgin if you will get me out of here. That's a promise. I swear it. I'll give you anything." Then she rather quickly put her fingers over her lips as if wondering whether she should have said what she did.

Without responding to her proposal, I turned to another woman who was waiting for a chance to speak. She was tall, thin, and feeble, with a dark complexion. Sensing that she was distressed, I found a place and suggested that we sit down together. She took a seat, looking about nervously.

Omitting the formality of introducing herself, she began, "I hurt in here," placing her hand on her chest. "I'm so depressed. I have nothing to look forward to except my misery. I can't stand this place. If I had known it was like this, I never would have come here." She gave a moan, then continued, her hands folded against her chest in prayer, "Oh, Lord, I've prayed and prayed and got no better. Oh, Lord, help me." Then turning to me, she said, "If I could only see someone besides these people who are here; they are not doing anything for anybody here." She began to groan again. "I've prayed and prayed to get well and go home and die there. That's all I want from life. I don't want to die here in this crazy house. I know I'll die when my time comes. I'd just as soon die tonight and get out of my misery." Then, looking into my eyes, she asked, "Chaplain, how does a person die?"

"I don't know," I replied. "I've never tried to die."

She smiled wistfully and spoke softly, "I lay down on my bed last night and tried to die, but I couldn't."

As I nodded my head, I thought to myself, If someone is as miserably unhappy as this woman is, what's against wishing one could die?

She continued in her weak voice, "I have passed through a severe bereavement in the death of my husband. It seems that the light of my life has gone out. Life seems completely empty. I don't want to live anymore. It seems impossible to continue to live."

Of course the world around this woman was the same as it had been before, but to her eyes it was dark and hopeless. In her grief her soul was so numbed by shock that she could see neither light nor feel any joy or interest in everyday things. I sat immersed in these thoughts for several minutes. Later I learned that this lady had once been a missionary to China with her husband.

A young brunette was sitting nearby. She wore a sullen, determined expression on her face. Several times she had pulled her dress up far above her knees, only to have one of the older women snatch it back into its proper place with a scolding remark, such as, "Jean, keep your dress down! Don't you have any decency? Don't you know that's the preacher? What kind of scene are you trying to make?"

As I rose from talking with the bereaved woman, I turned and asked, "Jean, why do you want to show your legs?"

"'Cause my mother didn't want me to," she replied rather bluntly without looking up.

I studied her. "Jean, you have beautiful legs. If I had legs that beautiful, I would want to show them too. God made them that way. You have a right to be proud of them." Looking up at me, Jean's eyes met mine and she smiled a sweet smile with gratitude all through it.

The plump woman with rosy cheeks who had propositioned me stepped close and smilingly said, "Forgive me if I said something to you that I shouldn't have said." I returned her smile, saying simply, "Of course, I forgive you."

A patient asked to speak privately with me. We went to one of the visiting rooms and she told me that she was a lesbian and asked me to listen to her story. Not having any knowledge about how to counsel lesbians, mine was mostly a listening part. She was greatly obsessed with her problem. I felt that I was not helpful to her.

"Chaplain."

I had returned to the disturbed ward. The voice seemed familiar.

"I'm glad you have come on our ward. I am Edith Collin." With that she extended her hand. "I believe I remember seeing you at the desk out front when I came this morning, or rather when those deputy sheriffs brought me in," she said, trying to be pleasant. "Weren't you standing out there?"

"Yes, I was there. I was waiting for Dr. Rivers, your doctor."

"Could I talk with you somewhere away from these folks?" she asked. I inquired of the ward attendant if this could be arranged. We went down the hall to Mrs. Collin's bedroom and entered. After closing the door, she sat on the bed and I sat on the only chair in the room.

"This is my room," she explained. Her room, like most of them on the ward, had only a single bed and a chair. There was no mirror and the walls were bare. Someone had written on the wall with lipstick the words "God is here." Looking up at the writing, she remarked, "I hope it's so, but I'm not so sure." She shook her head sadly. The next moment she broke into tears and hid her face on her knees. Then, raising her head, Mrs. Collin grasped my hand in hers and tried to smile through her tear-dimmed eyes, but it was an unsuccessful attempt. There was a defeated look in her reddened eyes. Her lips were white and trembling as she spoke in a low voice, saying, "This is a terrible thing my husband has done to me. I had no idea it was going to happen. This is a terrible shock to me. Those deputy sheriffs just brought me here and dropped me like I was a murderer."

The tears began to run down her cheeks. She reached for a handkerchief but had none, so she leaned her body over and reached for her slip, but there was none, so she used the hem of the dress the state had provided. Having wiped the tears away, she continued in a halting voice, "I don't see any reason for my being here. My husband evidently knew what I was getting into. I don't feel I was treated quite fair. They won't let me use the telephone. I have no choices. If I could use the phone I'd call my parents in Florida. They'd get me out of here. They've got influence."

After a brief pause, the brokenhearted woman continued, "If there is a God, why did he let this happen to me? Why did he desert me? I don't see that I deserve this." She buried her head in her palms and cried again, her body trembling. Then, wiping the tears away with the backs of her hands, she continued, "This is the darkest day in my life. I've suffered a lot but never like this. I didn't do anything to be put here. All my life I've tried to be good. This seems unreasonable. It's punishment to me."

I waited, not speaking. As her lips continued to tremble with emotion, I put my hand on her arm and pressed it. Brushing the hair out of her face with both hands, she tried to pull herself together. Her reddened eyes looked at nothing in particular as she spoke. "My husband and I have been married 12 years. We have three children. They go to school. They need me to get them ready every morning. My husband can't cook a lick."

After a moment, still looking at nothing, she continued, "It seemed like everything was going fine. Then a terrible thing happened. Another woman came into my husband's life. I didn't know anything about it until my parents told me. He made it so hard on them they moved back to Florida where I was born."

After slowly shifting her position on the bed, she spoke again. "I guess I pressed my husband too much about it instead of forgiving him. I should have let the matter drop. Every time I would say anything about the other woman, he'd call me a crazy woman. Finally, to save face and his business, he put me here. I guess he was trying to prove I was crazy, so it wouldn't hurt his business. He just wanted me out of the way. I was embarrassing to him."

"Mrs. Collin," I said, "whenever we are hurt in any way, that is the time for us to turn our thoughts from our hurts to God, our loving father who understands the way we feel. It's not easy to do, but it is necessary." I paused long enough for this thought to sink in, then continued, "Let us sit here together for a few moments and be silent in his presence, with our eyes closed. Let God heal the hurt that has come into your life."

A new comfort seemed to encircle the two of us. There was no asking God to do anything. After a brief silence, I rose and so did she. I was wondering if this woman really did belong here. Perhaps there should be some investigation. Hers was a believable story and could well be true. At the same time, I knew there could be another side to her story.

As I walked to the sitting room with her, Mrs. Collin said, smiling, "I feel better now. Do come back to see me soon."

Again, I entered the ward and found myself face to face with Sharon. "You again?" she asked in a sarcastic tone. Then she added, "If you're such a good Christian, or such a big Christian, get me out of here."

"Sharon, I've never thought of myself as a big or good Christian," I answered calmly.

Looking at the keys hanging from my belt, Sharon asked, "Do you preach against locked doors?"

"I don't preach for or against locked doors," I stated in a soft voice. "That's not my job."

"What are you doing with those keys anyway? Do you mean

you've got all these women locked up here? I suppose you think that's Christian? Shame on you!" She spoke defiantly, then added with an upturned nose, "I don't trust preachers or doctors. They are all cheats."

Usually two attendants worked on the ward, but a lone attendant was momentarily in charge of these 50 women. The other had gone to help prepare the noonday meal. The remaining attendant took her position between Sharon and me.

Suddenly Sharon stepped around the attendant and gave me a slap on the face which resounded loudly throughout the ward. I looked at her, stunned. One of the women gasped, "Oh, she shouldn't have done that." Some came to me and said, "I'm sorry she did that to you." The attendant explained apologetically, "I knew she was upset and might hit you. That's why I tried to stay between you and her. Are you all right?"

I rubbed my cheek with my hand since it was still smarting from the blow. I wondered why Sharon was so antagonistic toward me.

Several weeks later she would approach me when I was on her ward and ask, "Do you remember how mean I talked to you when you first came here?"

"Yes, I remember."

"Do you know why I talked to you like that?"

"No, but I'd like to know."

"My mother is a very religious woman. I hate her and I was just taking it out on you."

A woman drew nearer and spoke, "Chaplain, one of the women here tried to slander you. She said you got into trouble with a woman and they turned you out of the church. She said that's why you are working here, that you are an outcast. Is it true?"

"No, not a word of it is true," I replied.

"I don't know why she wanted to tell anything like that. I knew it wasn't true and you would tell me the truth. It was nothing but a lie. You've been faithful to your wife, haven't you?"

"Yes, I have for these 24 years and I plan to be so long as I live," I said.

"Dinner, ladies," called the attendant who had been helping with the preparation of the meal. Immediately most of the 50 women got up and started down the long hallway to the dining room. They moved haltingly, some as if in a daze. A few in wheelchairs were pushed by other women on the ward. Some were so feeble they had to be assisted. Several of the women crowded around me on their way and expressed their appreciation for my visit and asked me to come back to see them. I promised that I would. Some asked me to stay and eat dinner with them. I wondered what the meal was like and thought to myself, This is another way to identify with these troubled souls. I conferred with the attendant and received permission to eat with them.

I offered my arm to an elderly lady, letting her lean on me as we walked. She smiled in gratitude and introduced herself. "I'm Annie Hagler. There's nothing wrong with my mind; I'm just old. I am 74. When one gets old and can't wait on themselves, you can expect to be put anywhere, even here in the crazy house. Everyone here is sweet to me, but it hurts for my children to chuck me away like this."

After I had helped her to her seat at the table, the attendant placed me at the end of one of the two long tables which stretched across the room. When all the women were seated, Mrs. Norwood asked me to give thanks to God for the food. Some had started eating, but stopped. They looked at me expectantly. Almost all heads were bowed reverently for the brief prayer.

The meal consisted of meat loaf, turnip greens, creamed potatoes, banana pudding, milk and bread. Some applied themselves at once to eating; some just looked down or gazed out the window without eating; others who were unable to feed themselves were spoon-fed by an attendant. Only a spoon was allowed; there was no knife or fork. There were no napkins on the table since they too could be used to inflict harm.

"Sit down and eat your meal, Mrs. Jones," said a nurse to an elderly woman who had gotten up and was wandering around the room. Mrs. Jones shook her head violently.

"I don't want anything to eat," she replied. "I want to get out of here and go home. I didn't come here for a checkup. I didn't come here for anything," she added, raising her voice a bit. She had walked to the door. As the nurse approached, Mrs. Jones grabbed at the locked door, saying with some irritation, "Let me out of here. I've got to go home. You don't understand— my son is waiting out front for me."

The nurse said gently but firmly, "No, Mrs. Jones, you can't go home now," and with that she turned her around and led her to a place at the table.

After she was seated, Mrs. Jones looked around and said, "This is the darnedest hospital and the darnedest people." Then gazing out the window, she remarked, "I've just got to get out and look for my boy. He's out there somewhere; he's waiting for me." There was great urgency in her voice.

Still looking out the window, she continued, "When I leave this hospital, I'll never put my foot in here again. This is the worst place I've ever seen. It's an absolute disgrace. They've treated me dirty. I've been in lots of hospitals but never in one like this. They keep the door locked. They've got me locked up like I was a prisoner. I'm no criminal, I haven't done anything to be here. I'm a good woman. Just ask anyone. You ask my boy and he'll tell you it's so."

Distressed, Mrs. Jones spoke to no one in particular. Then gazing down at her wrist, she asked, "Where's my watch and ring? I guess those darn nurses took them off. They'll do any-thing. They stole them. I wouldn't put it past them."

A woman sitting nearby said, "Mrs. Jones, they put your watch and ring up so you won't lose them while you're here."

"I'm not going to stay here. I've got to go home," was her retort. "My boy—I can't keep him waiting. I can't stay."

The other woman said, "Yes, you will stay. I've been here six times. You'll stay."

"I'll bet I don't. I want to get my watch and my ring. My husband gave them to me." The attendant came and sat down beside her and said, "Mrs. Jones, go ahead now and eat your dinner," which she finally did.

One of the women said to me, "It must take a good deal of nerve for a man to be a chaplain in a place like this. I congratulate you."

Another said, "I wouldn't think any more so than anywhere else."

I responded, "I don't know yet, but it looks like I will have plenty to do."

I had already conferred with the nurse about the advisability of having a very brief devotional service when the meal was completed. I stood up and asked all who would to recite the Twenty-third Psalm with me. Many did so. Many knew it from memory—more than I had expected.

Then I spoke to them.

"Ladies, I appreciate the privilege of visiting with you today and of eating this noonday meal with you. I am here to help you any way I can while you are here with us. I have come to tell you that God loves you; each of you is precious to God. God loves us not because we are good, not because we are bad; he loves us because God is love.

"Some of you are wondering why you are here. You feel there has been some injustice. I don't know why you are here. Perhaps some of you are here because you are afraid and are trying to run away from something very important in life. Some may be trying to escape from life and its responsibilities, or from God, or from yourselves. Others may be here for some other reason that no one can tell. Wherever we are, God is with us. Remember, there is nothing whatsoever that can separate us from the love of God. He is here with us, even in our darkest hours."

While I was speaking, a tall, massive woman, weighing about 200 pounds and with a sprinkle of gray in her hair, stood near a window holding her hands above her head and looking at the ceiling. When I stopped talking, she came to me, slammed her right fist firmly against my chest and said, "Do you want to fight?"

"No, not today," I replied, smiling. She smiled too and walked away.

As the women were going back to the ward, the attendant came to me and said, "Mrs. Montgomery heard your voice and wants to talk with you. She is locked in her room. Would you like to see her?" I agreed and followed the attendant. Unlocking the door, she said, "Mrs. Montgomery, this is Chaplain Thomas." Greetings were exchanged and the attendant left. Mrs. Montgomery lay on her bed, her entire body trembling.

"I'm so nervous," she began. "I feel like I want to run away. I am afraid I will hurt myself. If anyone ever needed a padded cell, I feel that I do. Something's got to be done with me. I have to hold myself to keep from crushing myself against the wall."

"We have no padded cells," I explained.

There was a long pause during which tears rolled down her cheeks. She disregarded them except for an occasional brush with her hand. "I've been a good woman all my life," she continued. "I must have done something bad and God is punishing me for it. That's the only explanation for what has happened."

I thought to myself, She thinks God has put her here and is whipping her. I had known many people who looked upon illness as a punishment from God. This was a quite common belief. I had heard them say, "I guess God is angry with me." I could not accept such thinking.

"Mrs. Montgomery," I said, "You say you've tried to be a good woman all your life. You have children, I suppose."

"Yes, I have three."

"Let's look at it this way. If we love our children, we will not punish them when they are doing their best to be good, will we?"

"No, I guess not."

"Then, should we believe God would punish you after you

have tried to be a good person?" I asked. "Would that make any sense?"

"No, I suppose I was wrong," was her reply.

"Mrs. Montgomery, you need to remember that God loves you. When you turn to him for help, you will find the help you need. If I care, and the doctor, nurse and attendants care, how much more does God care for you? His love and caring are boundless, but ours are limited by our humanity."

As I was leaving her room, I asked, "Shall I lock your door?"

"Yes, please do. I don't want to be bothered by any of the patients coming in. They're always bothering me."

As I came out of the room, the attendant said, "We have another woman in here I wish you would see." Unlocking another door, the attendant said, "Mrs. Thompson, here's someone to see you." There was no movement. The woman was in her bed, covered up with a blanket, her face to the wall.

"Mrs. Thompson, the chaplain wants to talk with you," called the attendant again. Slowly the large woman turned her head, squinting her eyes as she adjusted them to the light. Looking me over, she finally said slowly and softly, "My head aches awfully. I don't feel much like talking to anyone." The attendant left the room.

"Mrs. Thompson, I am Chaplain Thomas. I heard you were here. I would like for us to get acquainted. I may be able to help you."

"Close that door," she requested. "Have a chair. You are not afraid of me, are you?" She still spoke slowly. "A lot of people are afraid of me."

"No, of course not," I replied a bit dubiously.

"I didn't expect to find a chaplain here. Circumstances brought me here, family troubles. My husband was once a preacher. Now he's an alcoholic. He won't ever come here to see me. He put his mother here but never would come to see her. I came several times to see her."

The woman turned all the way over in her bed so that she

faced me, then continued, "My husband has been planning for two years to do this to me. It was the primary thing on his mind. They lied to me. I sang in the choir in my church. It hurts, it hurts, it hurts," she moaned, her voice rising with increasing anguish. She sobbed and wiped at the tears running down her cheeks. "The way they lied to me! It destroyed all my confidence."

She stopped sobbing and continued, "They tricked me into going to the jail. My preacher didn't have to. My husband didn't have to. They promised to come back to the jail to see me, but didn't. I looked and looked and looked for them but they never came. The truth is, they just left me here. No, they didn't have to lie to me."

"Mrs. Thompson, do you feel that you need to be here?"

"I need to be here or somewhere. My God, my God, God, why?" she cried, sobbing heavily again. Gaining control of her voice, she looked me over and remarked, "You seem to be a real nice person. Are you a chaplain, sure enough, or was that another lie? I'm so tired of lies."

"Yes, Mrs. Thompson, I'm the chaplain."

"I don't know why I'm telling you all this."

"You needed to tell someone, Mrs. Thompson. That's why I'm here, so you can tell me."

"I guess my husband got tired of looking at me. He must have put me here so he could run around with other women 'cause there is nothing wrong with my mind. If I'm crazy now, then I was crazy when he married me. I haven't changed any since then. I've got as good a mind as I've ever had." After a brief pause, she continued, "I need a headache pill, but they haven't given me one. I need an aspirin more than I need to cry on the chaplain's shoulder. I haven't had a bite of food since yesterday. I'm getting pretty hungry. Could I have something to eat?"

"I will tell the attendant. I'm sure they will bring you a tray. I must go now. I'm glad to know you, Mrs. Thompson. If I can help you any way, feel free to call on me."

"I already feel much better since talking to you," she replied. "If you had not come today, I think I would have been stark crazy by tomorrow." She seemed to gaze at me with fondness and gratitude.

As I started up the hall toward the sitting room, a woman came out of the bathroom. Without giving her name, she said, "Chaplain, I'd like to talk with you, if you have time." There was a pleading look in her eyes.

Without hesitating, I replied, "Yes, we can talk. Let's step into this room."

She began without any prompting. "You said in your talk after lunch that we wondered why we are here. I know why I'm here. It's not because I'm sick in the head, but I'm sick in the soul. I've done lots of things I shouldn't and now I recognize what they were."

The woman was attractive, although her dark hair needed combing. She lowered her head and looked at the floor as she continued her confession. "My husband died. I had to do what I did for a while, or thought I had to in order to make a living for my children. Then it got to be a habit. Pretty soon, I didn't even think about it. I've lived with this man almost five years. He supported me and my children, but I knew he had a wife and two sons at home. His wife didn't believe in divorces. She got a divorce from bed and board, but not a complete divorce. That's what she wanted."

For a few moments she sat there brushing at the front of her institutional dress, smoothing out the wrinkles. "I couldn't go home to my people," she continued, still looking at the floor. "They'd let me come, but I didn't want to go. I thought about it and thought about it, and got to worrying. I don't want to live like that anymore. I couldn't take him with me. I don't want my people to be ashamed of me. I don't want my children to be ashamed of me. Since coming here, I've seen so many people so much worse than I am physically, but not any could be any worse than I am spiritually."

THROUGH THESE EYES

Looking again at the ill-fitting dress provided by the hospital, she said apologetically, "I'm wearing borrowed clothes. I didn't pick this outfit out. This dress stinks. I guess I'm in sackcloth and ashes for the sins I've done."

I didn't say that she was a bad woman. I didn't condemn, criticize, or judge her. That would not help. Furthermore, that was not my way. I didn't try to bring about a change in this woman's habits, behavior or personality. I replied softly, "Perhaps you remember the words of Jesus. He said to a woman taken in the act of adultery, 'Neither do I condemn thee: go, and sin no more.'"* I laid my hand on her shoulder.

Slowly the woman lifted her face, looking unwaveringly into mine for the first time. She smiled a pretty smile as she reached for my hand. Holding it in both of hers, she said, "Thank you, chaplain. You have helped me." There were tears of joy flowing down her face. She had not told her name and that was unimportant to me.

As I unlocked the screen door separating us from the sitting room, I saw another woman standing there as if waiting for a chance to talk with me.

"May I speak with you?" she asked. I nodded and took her arm, leading her into the same room I had just used. The patient sat down with her hands resting in her lap but said nothing. There were severe lines around her mouth, her eyes were expressionless, her cheeks pale, and her shoulders slumped. Then she bowed her head and covered her face with her hands as if trying to shut everything out. Stunned and bewildered, she sat there.

Waiting, I remembered her as the woman who had made a scene at the receptionist's desk, tearing up the commitment papers and throwing her rings across the lobby. With the change

---

* John 8:11, King James Version

THROUGH THESE EYES

from her elegant clothes to these state clothes, and her broken spirit, she did not look anything like the person who had come through the front door with her husband. Yes, this was Mrs. Martha Richardson. And she was obviously in a sorrowful state.

Finally, she lifted her head, placing her fingers on her trembling lips. Looking at me, she tried to smile as she wiped her moist eyes with the backs of her hands. Then she lowered her eyes and gazed at her ring finger. Again, tears rolled. "They wouldn't let me wear my wedding rings," she began. "That's the first time in my married life that they've been off my hand. It feels so peculiar. How can God let such things happen to us?"

Her sobs were dreadful, racking her whole body. I patted her arm gently but remained silent. Mrs. Richardson straightened up and looked around her, then continued. "I don't know why I'm here," she said, her lips still quivering. "My husband and I have had some trouble. I guess all people do. It's perfectly natural, happens in every marriage. But we've never been separated. I can't stand this. I've not committed any crime. I've never done anything to be here."

I was silent as I studied the woman. "I can't have my rings," she went on. "I was given this old, smelly institutional dress. I feel I've been stripped of all my dignity. My husband told me he was bringing me here to this city to see my grandchildren, and by here for a checkup. My son is here at the university. It hurts my pride to be here. It's my husband who did wrong when he got interested in another woman. I told him I'd do something. I didn't say what. I didn't say whether I'd scratch his eyes out or shoot him. I can't even shoot a gun.

"Can't we defend our homes?" she asked. "Can't we stand up for our rights?" Her voice became sharper as she spoke. Without waiting for a reply to her questions, she continued, "I guess none of us think there's anything wrong with us. We all feel we don't belong here, but I'm being punished for something he's done. He's the one who ought to be here and take the punishment." She squeezed her reddened eyes shut as if trying to hold back the tears. "How can one whom I have loved and trusted for 25 years put me here? How do you explain that, chaplain? I've given my husband the best years of my life and now he puts me here." The tears began to trickle down her cheeks, but she ignored them.

"Two weeks ago my husband slapped me several times and said he'd put me here and leave me for the rest of my life. He said no one could take me out of here but him and he said he'd be damned if he'd ever take me out. He said I'd crouch in the corner and stare out into space and rot. He said that's what I deserve. He said he'd take the children and I'd never see them again."

I shook my head sadly. Brushing the tears away, Mrs. Richardson continued, "I have a grandson born a month ago. It will be awful for it to go down on his record that his grandmother has been in a place like this." Then turning to me, she asked, "Can you tell me why my husband did this to me? Why am I here?"

"Mrs. Richardson," I explained, "someone thought you needed to come and stay here a while. A doctor and a probate judge in your county had to sign the commitment papers before your husband could bring you here."

"I've not been to a doctor in nearly a year and the probate judge has never seen me. How can a doctor do that when he hasn't seen me? What kind of frame-up is that? They are supposed to be ethical. I'm not resentful. I'm just hurt. I'm crushed in two ways. I've heard of these things happening, but I've never really believed it. Does the law mean no more than that? I don't understand."

"Your husband may have become afraid when you threatened him," I explained.

Mrs. Richardson continued, "I must have failed somewhere along the way or I wouldn't be here. If I tell the doctor about that other woman, he will give me those electric shock treatments. He'll think they will make me forget her. I don't believe in those shock treatments. I'd rather stay here than take shock treatments. I can't ever trust my husband anymore since he did this to me. How can I ever go back to him?

"When my husband and I came in the front door," she went on, "I acted up rather badly. It was because I was afraid. It was so unfair of my husband to trick me. Why did he lie? What made him do it?" Then she remembered, "I believe you were standing there." I nodded my head. "I'm sorry I acted up as I did," she said apologetically. After a moment's pause, Mrs. Richardson concluded, "Well, chaplain, I must not keep you any longer. I know you will be praying for me while I'm here."

I nodded soberly. "I certainly will, Mrs. Richardson. That is my sacred privilege."

As we walked toward the door, she said, "I just want to say that you are our best medicine. You are a godsend to us patients. I've been watching you today. I've observed that you treat everyone alike. Take that prostitute over there, for instance," she nodded in a patient's direction. "You treat her with the same courtesy you show the rest of us. That's as it should be, and I admire you for treating us all alike."

"Those are very kind words, Mrs. Richardson. This is the first day here for both of us. I want to do everything I can to be helpful."

As I was about to leave, a pretty brunette with a shapely figure came to me. Both wrists were bandaged, and I wondered if she had attempted suicide. Looking squarely into my eyes and trying to be pleasant, she said, "My name is Mary Jo Barker. I want to ask you a question. Are we disgraced because we are here?"

I replied thoughtfully, "Some people who come here do feel that way about it, and some of their relatives feel that way about it, too. I do not consider it any more a disgrace to come here than to go to any other hospital."

Another lady standing nearby remarked assuredly, "Just give the folks outside time enough and they'll be here too."

"I've had more peace in this ward since I came here than there was at home for three weeks before I came," said Mary Jo. Then she added, smiling, "You must be a mighty good man to come work with us here."

A woman interrupted by asking, "Are you a Communist?"

"No, I'm not. Why do you ask?"

She looked at me defiantly. "I believe you are 'cause of the way they do here on this ward." She walked away, leaving me to figure out what she meant. I crossed to the far side of the ward.

"Chaplain, how long is soon?"

The question was put to me by a thin, neat patient. "I'm sorry; I do not really know. Why do you ask?"

"Well, I just wondered. I asked the doctor this morning when I could go home. He said, 'Soon.' He told me the same thing six months ago and I am still here." I really did not know how to answer her.

As I passed on and drew nearer to another patient, she pulled off one of her shoes and threw it against the wall. I decided I had better move in another direction lest she throw the other one at me. I continued visiting with some other patients. Later, I encountered the shoe thrower again and she gave me a sly grin as we passed. I thought she had gone on, but suddenly she turned around and slapped me a hard lick on my left ear, then walked away. My ear burned for 20 or 30 minutes from the blow, or so it seemed.

I moved on to a more friendly group. One of these women said to me, "Chaplain, some of the women here say you are a whoremonger. You are not, are you?"

"No."

"I told them you were not any such thing. I told them you were a man of God."

I thanked her for setting them straight on this.

Lisa, a patient whom I recognized as a distant cousin of mine, approached with a distressed look on her face and asked me to pray for her. I agreed and she spontaneously knelt on the floor with her hands folded in prayer. I rested my hands lightly on her head and prayed, "God, our loving father, here is one of your dear ones. She needs your help. Bless her. Give her peace and help her to trust you." As I helped her rise from her knees, Lisa was all smiles.

As I started to move on, I noticed a woman sitting nearby with her head resting on her arms on a table. Her body was trembling slightly and I knew she was in tears. I went over to the table, sat beside her and talked quietly, trying to help.

Farther down the ward, I spoke to a woman sitting in a rocking chair. "And how is it with you today?"

"I'm tired."

"Tired? There in that rocker?"

"I'm tired of resting."

Another patient said, "Chaplain, do you love me?"

I was slow about how to answer. If I told her no it would be untrue, but I feared she might misinterpret a yes. As I hesitated, another patient turned to her and said, "Of course the chaplain loves you. He loves all of us patients."

A woman with an open Bible in her hand said, "Chaplain, you'll have to get on your knees and pray if you want to get away from all these hens," pointing toward the other women in the ward.

"Isn't there some other way to get out?" I asked jokingly.

"No, you will have to pray your way out," she answered seriously.

I looked at my watch and was surprised. The hours had passed quickly. Turning to the ladies, I explained that I must go but would be back soon. At that moment a young lady caught my hand and said, "My name is Jo. You remind me so much of my granddaddy. I love him so much." With that she reached up and planted a kiss on my cheek, then smiled as she stepped back. Another woman looked at Jo disapprovingly for kissing me. "Oh, it's no harm to kiss him," explained Jo. "He's a man of God." She giggled delightedly.

Finally, as I turned to leave, several women began to wave good-bye. Some said, "Good-bye, Chaplain Thomas." I waved back to them and turned my key quietly in the lock.

I walked erectly as I returned to my office. There I reflected upon the day's experiences. Each person I had met during the day had a different problem. Each person had challenged me. As I remembered an alcoholic woman, a drug addict, a prostitute, an unmarried girl five months pregnant, and all the others I had met, I remembered that these outcasts of society were the kinds of people with whom Jesus kept company. They were the rejects with whom he associated.

After the day's work, I had a slight headache and felt fatigued. Before leaving for home, I sat down in my chair, took a few deep breaths, then became still in the silence, knowing there was a presence with me which sustained and maintained my life. After a few minutes I had an unexpected and amazing experience. The nervous fatigue and headache were gone. I felt a warm glow within and was completely refreshed throughout my being. A great peace enveloped me.

I rose from my chair and left my office, locking the door behind me. Driving home, I felt a deep sense of satisfaction at having done my best. Clytie Mae met me at our door. We embraced and she asked, "What's it like being chaplain in a mental hospital?"

"Challenging!" I exclaimed.

That night I had trouble falling asleep. Pictures came into my mind of the women I had met. There was Sharon; there were Edith Collin, Lynn, Jo, Joleen, Mrs. Norwood, Martha Richardson, and all the rest telling their unhappy stories to me again. I could hear their sobs, groans and laughter echoing in my head. But I knew I must put these people out of my mind; it was important for me to get some sleep.

- 4 -

After Mrs. Martha Richardson had completed her
evening meal, she went to the sitting room and sat
down by another patient. Introducing herself, she
said, "My name's Martha Richardson. What's yours?"

"I'm Edith Collin. I saw you not long after you came in. I
had just gotten here a few minutes before you came." Then she
added, smiling, "I don't know why I'm here. I'm not insane at
all, are you?"

Martha shook her head and they both laughed. Then Edith
continued, "I was forced into this place. They did it without
any authority. There's nothing wrong with my mind and never
has been."

Martha Richardson looked around the room at the other
women and then said, "I know I'm not like most of these people
here. I've never gone blank. I'm not crazy either, but if I stay
here a month, I know what will happen. I'll be like the rest of
them. I sure don't want that to happen to me." Their conversation was almost a suppressed whisper.

Pointing to a buxom woman with heavily rouged cheeks,
Martha said, "She walks up and down the ward cursing. It's all
she's good for. I'm just not used to such things. I can't stand it

much longer. I have to get out of here. I'm on the verge of a crack-up." She paused a moment, then went on, "I don't know why my husband brought me here, but I'll know when I get home. I'll get the truth out of him, and soon." She spoke hopefully.

Anna Sanford passed by at that moment, overheard the remark, and spoke: "Don't be too sure of yourself, dear. That's what I thought too, but I've been here three months and that Dr. Rivers won't even discuss the possibility of my going home. All he thinks about is giving me those awful shock treatments."

Edith said, "When I think of what my husband has done to me, I almost feel like the woman who said, 'Damn all men!'"

"It isn't fair," Martha said. "My husband tricked me into coming here. He said we were coming down here to visit our grandchild. Our son is in the university. My husband suggested that since I'd been a little nervous, we stop off first for a checkup."

"These people here sure are mixed up," said Edith, glancing across the room at the women, some laughing for no apparent reason, others cursing or looking woebegone. Two of the younger ones were dancing together; one middle-aged woman was picking up straws from the floor and sticking them in her hair, seemingly oblivious to her surroundings; and another, not having presence of mind to go to the rest room, had wet on the floor. "Only a few can talk with any sense," continued Edith, "and all they talk about is drinking, fighting, or sex. They are all trash, as I see it," she said with disgust.

"Well, I'm no alcoholic or murderer and I know I'm no prostitute," Martha replied. Lowering her voice and looking around, she said, almost in a whisper, "There are two women on this ward who killed their children." Then raising her voice a bit, she continued, "I tell you, I just don't belong here. I'm a Christian."

Suddenly there was a clattering sound. A woman in a wheelchair had rolled herself in their direction and heard Martha say that she didn't belong in Bryce. She announced,

The design of the Main Building, first used in 1861, is symbolic of the mid-19th century move from inhumane asylums to "moral" treatment for the mentally ill.

"I don't belong here either." Raising her voice, she launched into her story. "Two deputy sheriffs got hold of me before I knew what they were doing. They just grabbed me like I was a hog. My two sons are looking for me. They don't know where I am. If they learn I'm here, they'll come get me. I don't deserve to be here. If I did, I wouldn't mind it." She pulled her dress up slightly, and showing a stump, she said, "See, my leg is cut off here. My husband is the cause of my being here. He sneaked around and did this to me because I wouldn't work. If he wanted me to work, he should have got me an artificial limb so I could work. But he never would do that."

Martha said understandingly, "Life wasn't supposed to be like this, was it?"

"Of course not," replied the woman in the wheelchair.

"I haven't any mental trouble," said Martha. "I've got as much up in the brain as I ever had. I used to be a school teacher."

"If I needed to be here, I would have known it," said Edith. "I would have got up and come on my own accord. They wouldn't have had to bring me. I know I wouldn't put my husband here. I'd love and care for him at home."

"I'm tired of looking at women all day with their meaning-less chatter, pacing back and forth on the ward and to the bath-room," Martha commented. "The nurse and attendants are nice enough but the rest of the people are terrible."

While all this was going on in the sitting room, Sharon sat apart. After completing her evening meal, she had asked the attendant for pencil and paper. She would write a letter to her mother. The young woman hated her parent and gave intense expression to her passion, pouring her virulence into every sen-tence, and finally closing the letter: "With no love at all—Sharon."

Sharon then joined a new acquaintance, Janie, a young, pimple-faced, 19-year-old mother. "I've been here a week and two days and that doctor hasn't talked to me yet, except he gave me a physical examination," Janie began. "When I try to talk to him, he gives me the same excuse: no time. If he doesn't have time to talk to me or let me talk to him about my headache and this hurting in my chest, I want a new doctor."

"Dr. Rivers, uh!" said Sharon, pretending to gag. "I can't stand him. He bugs me. I run and hide when I see him coming. They say he keeps you a long time. I have no use for him. He's too unreasonable. He's hard. He's as crazy as some of these sensible crazy folks." She laughed and, leaning toward Janie, said, "I'm miserable here. If I stay much longer, I will be as crazy as a bumblebee. I just don't belong in this place. There's nothing wrong with me except meanness." Saying this, she laughed again and Janie took it as a cue to join in.

Mrs. Sanford, who was sitting across the room, heard the remark and called out, "You can say that again, Sharon, but you can do better than you do." Sharon ignored Anna Sanford and turned back to her friend.

Janie spoke again, saying, "What worries me is that I want to get out of here before they start giving me shock treatments. Then they want to give me drugs. My mind is clear now, but it won't be if they start giving me shock." Pausing a moment, she went on, "I have a bad temper when my husband beats me up. But if he will get me out of here, I'll never say another cross word. I don't care if he kills me; even that would be better than this."

"Ladies, it's nine o'clock. Bedtime." It was the voice of the night ward attendant who had just looked up from her magazine. Several women had already gone to bed. Edith, Martha, Anna, and the woman in the wheelchair all moved toward the bathroom, then on to their rooms for the night. Sharon, Janie, and several others were still talking.

"Girls, I said it was bedtime. Hurry along, please." Reluctantly, they shuffled off to bed. The bedroom doors were locked for the night. Each had vertical wooden bars. There was one woman to a room and a chamber pot served as a makeshift toilet for the night. The hall lights shone through the bars to provide necessary illumination.

A great fear came over both Edith and Martha after they'd said good night and as they lay alone in their separate rooms. Down the hall an elderly patient rattled her door and yelled, "Nurse, nurse, I want some water."

Gradually, inevitably, finally, all eyes grew tired and closed.

- 5 -

On my second morning many questions raced through my mind as I entered the Men's Receiving Building (MRB). Are mentally ill men more difficult to work with than mentally ill women? How will they receive me? How can I convince them to let me help them?

I glanced hastily over the disturbed ward in the building, seeing despair, anguish, and worry in the faces of the patients. I felt the room was filled with hate, fear, and suspicion.

More than 40 men were on the ward, passing their time in a variety of ways. One lay on the floor sleeping; two gazed out the window; another indifferently played solitaire. Two men were at a game of checkers, another read a book, while four sat at a table playing dominoes. One fellow was reading his hometown paper, probably forwarded to him by his family; another was writing a letter home. Other men sat quietly in an adjacent room; occasionally one got up and went to the water fountain or the rest room. Several of the men sat dejectedly, their faces revealing their hopelessness. Many faces were blank.

"Fellows, this is Chaplain Thomas. He has come to work with us here at the hospital," the ward attendant announced in clipped tones.

I addressed everyone: "Fellows, I'll be around here a while. I'd just like to get acquainted with you." Only a few men looked up and scrutinized me.

Standing across the room near the wall, a man called out, hostile and resentful, "Chaplain, if this hospital needs you, then I need a steamboat." There was a ripple of laughter. I ignored the remark. Another patient turned to his neighbor and said in a loud whisper, "He must not be much of a preacher; otherwise, what would he be doing here? Doesn't he know we are all crazy?"

An old man, who did not bother to give his name, greeted me jovially. "I want to meet our chaplain." He added, "Chaplain, my folks say I am losing my mind. Maybe I am, but I ain't missed it yet." There was an amused expression on his face. He turned to another patient. "Say, don't you want to shake hands with the chaplain?" His question was directed to a surly fellow who was on his way to the water fountain.

"Hell, no! I'm not shaking hands with no damn preacher," the man muttered out of the corner of his mouth.

A nice looking young man dressed in pajamas had been slowly walking the floor. He stopped, extended his hand and said, "I am Abraham Lincoln." He then resumed his pacing up and down the ward, chuckling slightly from time to time.

The old man's expression turned serious. "I've got no business here in this place, chaplain. My wife sent me down here. They said I was crazy, but if I am crazy, then I've been crazy 57 years. My mind is as good as it ever was. I was working when they brought me here."

I took a seat among the men, gratified that I'd gained their attention. They stopped playing checkers and dominoes. The newspaper and book were laid aside. Most of those who had been listless showed some interest. They looked at me expectantly, but I tried to speak as little as possible, preferring to let the fellows get things off their chests.

The man who had been reading spoke. "Chaplain, I am

Buddy Allen. I came willingly to the hospital in the hope that they could help me. I've been here three weeks and haven't seen a doctor yet except for about five minutes when I arrived. He gave me a physical examination."

I knitted my eyebrows. "I do not know why the doctor has not seen you, Mr. Allen, but I do know he has about 200 men to look after. He also has to see many visitors and he has a heavy correspondence answering letters from the families who write to ask how you fellows are getting along." I recognized the possibility that the man had been seen by the doctor but had forgotten, for the doctor tried to make his rounds on the wards every day.

"I don't mean to make fun of this place," said a young man with a shrug of his shoulders and a twitch of his face, "but if I stay here much longer, I'll be crazy. I'll be counting bugs on the walls. There's nothing wrong with my mind. I just want my freedom."

I learned later the identity of this young man. His name was J. R. Gardner. He was tall, slender, sandy-haired, and only 19 years old. He had been born out of wedlock to a mother who went off and left him for his grandmother to rear. When her health failed and she could no longer cope with the child, she placed him in an orphanage. He had not gotten along well there. Incorrigible, he was placed in a boy's reform school. From there he was sent to a state school for retarded children, and eventually sent to Bryce.

The silence following J. R.'s comment was broken by a handsome man who explained, "Chaplain, let me tell you my problem: a nervous breakdown caused by overwork. I needed the treatment, and believe me, I have received much personal attention while here. I know the doctor likes to see his patients get well and go home. I feel I am well now. I need to get back to my family; besides, I miss my job. I work at a rubber plant and am losing $16 a day while I'm here. I feel I'm cured now."

"Would you like to tell us what lesson you have learned since you came here for treatment?" I asked.

"I don't mind," he replied readily. "I've learned the human body is not a machine. The body must have proper rest and, moreover, a person must eat regularly. A healthy body makes for a healthy mind. We need a great spiritual mind. If we don't have that, we will have a criminal mind." He sat down and I thanked him for sharing his thoughts.

"I'm 87 years old," spoke another man in a feeble, cracked voice. "This is the first time in my life I've been locked up. They call me crazy. If I'm crazy, well, I guess I was born that way. I'm living with my third wife. That is where I made my mistake. I should never have married that woman. She has been hard on me. I tried to get out of it the easy way."

"And what was the easy way, sir?" I asked.

Pointing to his bandaged neck, the elderly patient replied, "I tried to cut it." After a pause, he continued, "If it had not been for my wife, I would not be in this predicament. She put me here so she could get her hands on my savings. I should never have married her."

A man in his late thirties said, "Chaplain, I've been here seven weeks. I'm worried about losing my car and my television set. I owe $1,800 on the car. I'm perfectly sane. They are keeping me here because of my drinking. This will never cure me of drinking. If anything, it only makes me want to drink worse. Worrying about money I've put into the car and TV set is enough to drive a man to liquor." After a pause, he asked, "Chaplain, can you help me get out of here so I can take care of these things?"

"Of course, I want to help any way I can," I replied. "That's why I'm here among you. But I have no authority to send you back home. That is the responsibility of the doctor."

Crossing his legs, resting his hands on his lap, and wearing an expression of utter futility, he continued, "I had a good home, a good job and a fine family. I've made a mess of my life. Now I've lost my home, my wife and children, and my job. And probably my TV and car as well. Here I am locked up in the crazy house and I can't do a thing about it."

In an attempt to offer a ray of hope to this man and to the others who were sitting there, I said, "My friend, you say you have messed up your life, and things do look rather bad for you. There are times when only God can untangle the mess we have made of our lives, but sometimes the help comes from some unexpected source, even the doctor."

"You can make heaven or hell out of being here," said Bill Kirksey, a stocky, well-built young man with dark crew-cut hair. He had been a silent but interested listener until now. "I myself have few complaints. I have plenty to eat and everyone is nice. Please don't blame the hospital. There's nothing wrong with my mind—only my soul. I've done wrong and I know it. I was a drinker. I tried to drown my troubles by drinking. I drank so much whisky I had to come here for treatment. I've paid dearly for my folly; in fact, I'm still paying. What I need is God's forgiveness."

As he spoke, it was plain to see that Bill's soul was hungry for inner satisfaction. He longed for happiness but did not understand where true happiness lies. He had looked for happiness where he thought it could be found but the result was only further confusion and unhappiness. I found that his was a common case.

J. R. Gardner spoke again. "I like the food. They feed us plenty, but chaplain, this is a living hell. It's an ungodly hellhole, and it's lousy with murderers."

Some of the men turned unkindly glances toward J. R., in obvious disagreement with that remark. I cleared my throat. "I've been trying to imagine myself in your place. I think I can understand, at least in a measure, how you feel about being away from your families and your jobs. Certainly we all miss home. There's no place like it. It is clear that some of you feel like it is hell to be here in the hospital. But do you know that even the deepest hell can prove to be a gateway to heaven if we turn and become aware of God and his love? Try to realize his loving presence right here, even in the midst of this place. This is worth thinking about, fellows. Now suppose we close our eyes for a few moments of silent prayer." The men complied. After several seconds I broke the silence by saying, "It's been good being with you fellows. I'll be seeing you again soon." I rose to my feet, only to be interrupted.

"Chaplain, before you go, may I ask you a question?" A neatly dressed old man spoke in a soft and plaintive voice. "You preachers say we are all here because of some evil we have done. I beg to disagree. As a young man I lived a clean life. I've never drunk, gambled, cursed and the like. I've never touched any woman but my wife. I've been faithful to my church and supported it financially to the best of my ability. Yet you claim I've done evil."

The old fellow and the others leaned forward expectantly. "My friend, yours is a good question," I replied. "I'm not sure I can answer it to your satisfaction or mine. I do not recall in my life ever having said that all the people here are here because they have done wrong. That is too simple an explanation. However, I have heard some preachers make that sort of statement. In fact, I am a different kind of preacher, if you want to call me a preacher. I do not preach damnation and hellfire; I am interested in the love of God.

"I do not condemn those who come here; I do not blame anyone for being sick. I do not say that one has been naughty or has violated the laws of life. The fact is that the person has suffered and that is enough. Our mistakes of the past are not important to God. They are important to us only because they can teach us lessons which we need to learn, so we will not repeat the same mistakes again. I am here to help in any way I can. If I can help you, feel free to call upon me. I am always available to speak with you."

Several men stepped forward as I was leaving. "Thank you, chaplain, for coming our way."

An activity room such as this was located on most wards in the 1950's.

"God surely sent you to us."

"You certainly have given a lift to our spirits."

Bill Kirksey said, "Fellows, the chaplain is the best medicine for us patients."

A young man approached me in the hall. "Chaplain, I need to talk to you if you can spare the time."

"All right. Let's step into this room where we will not be interrupted," I answered. The youth seemed shy and I prodded him to speak. "What is your trouble?"

"Briefly, it's this. I am an only child. I was born six months after my parents were married. For as long as I can remember, my father has pointed an accusing finger at me and said, 'You are not my child, but I've got to feed you.' My mother didn't want me either; she sent me to live with my aunt. After getting my two years of military training, I married an orphan girl. I overindulged in sex until my wife got disgusted and threatened to leave me. I made life intolerable for her. I knew I needed help so I asked to come here. My wife is pregnant and is staying with my parents. I'm afraid my daddy will beat her up because he has beat me up many times when he was drinking. He drinks nearly all the time."

"How do you think I can help you?" I wondered aloud.

"Couldn't you write my pastor to see if my wife is being taken care of? She has no relatives living that she can stay with. If she is being mistreated, maybe my pastor can arrange for her to stay at The Salvation Army home while I'm doing my time here."

I nodded, "I'll certainly do that for you."

As I came out of the room, an elderly man said to me, "Chaplain, my name is Perkins. I want to make a request of you. It may sound crazy, but I want to write my wife. The problem is I don't know how. It's been over 40 years since I wrote a letter. I've never had any reason to do so and I've forgot how to write a letter. I wish you would show me how to start it." I sat down and helped him write the letter.

Just as we finished, a young patient approached me and said, "I like it here. I came here from the penitentiary, and you may not believe what I'm going to tell you. The men in the pen think it's so much better here that they do all sorts of things trying to prove themselves crazy. They eat cockroaches and get down on their knees and drink urine from the latrine."

"Do they prove their insanity and get to come here?"

"No, the authorities know they're just pretending to be nuts."

Another man, after giving his name, said, "I would like to speak to you privately." We went to his bedroom. Sitting on the side of the bed, he said, "My life is ruined, chaplain." Despite his efforts to speak calmly, he was obviously in great distress. "I killed a man in the next county and I'm here for observation to determine my sanity. I'm possibly facing the electric chair. I am 50 years old with a good wife and three children. Who will take care of them? If I'm declared insane, I guess I'm here for the rest of my days. If I'm not declared insane, I guess I will be in the penitentiary for the rest of my days. I want you to pray for me and my family."

I nodded understandingly. "That will be a privilege. I am with you in prayer." Then we prayed together, thanking God that he is still with us regardless of what happens to us and that he cares for us and our loved ones.

Another man waiting near the door beckoned me to come to him. He whispered, "If I could get something to do it with, I would pluck out my eyes."

"Why do you want to do that?"

He looked at me as if I were foolish. "Doesn't the Bible say if a man looks upon a woman and lusts after her, it would be better if his eyes were plucked out?"

"Yes," I admitted.

"Well, I saw a nude woman, and I lusted after her, and I feel I should punish myself by plucking out my eyes."

"Let's stop and think a minute," I said, trying to be helpful. "Do you have children?"

"Yes, I have four."

"Would you want to see someone put their eyes out?"

"No, I wouldn't," replied the man.

"Isn't God a lot better than you or I?"

"Sure, he is."

"Well, God created your eyes. He doesn't go around poking out people's eyes, and I don't believe he wants us to do so either." I was hesitant, doubting if my words would alleviate the man's guilt.

Still another man came forward. "I'd like to talk with you if you can spare the time. I'm a minister. I feel that I've been railroaded here. I got involved with the law. It was because of my wife and kids. I wanted to see them. We haven't lived together for two years. She was at her mother's. She had told me to stay away. When I went to the house, she called the law. I resisted arrest and tried to outrun them. They were like wild men and shot 17 times into the back of my car. One of the cops had been dating my wife. They threw me into jail and then brought me here. I feel there has been a serious miscarriage of justice."

"So you feel that you were handed a rough deal, don't you?" I remarked.

"I sure do." Clasping my hand, he said, "Pray for me." As I prayed, I could hear him quietly sobbing. When the brief prayer was concluded, he dropped his head on my shoulder and let the tears flow. "Just think," said he, "how miserably I have failed." He sobbed more. "Just think—I have fallen from the ministry to this."

"Remember, my brother," I said, trying to be consoling, "no man has failed in life until he refuses to pick himself up and try again. That is the only failure. God has not made us to be failures, but conquerors." I held his hand for a moment, then walked toward the ward door.

A man called, "Chaplain." I waited for him. "Chaplain, they can put locks on the doors and bars on those windows but they can't keep God out of a mental hospital."

"Yes, you are right. Wherever we are, God is. Even though we make our bed in hell or in a mental hospital, God is with us. He has promised never to leave us or forsake us." Smiling, I clasped this man's hand, then turned the key in the door and walked down the corridor. I thought to myself, How nearly normal most of these men seem to be! A very thin line separates me from them, but I thank God I'm still on the outside.

I entered an untidy ward where I found many of the patients lying on their beds. Mr. Smith, a former minister, lay on his waterproof bed cover in a puddle of urine. When I inquired how he was getting along he replied, "This is heaven. If it is not heaven, it is the gateway to heaven."

Near him lay another man, also obviously wet. I asked him how things were and he answered, "This is hell." I asked an attendant why the men were lying there wet and I was told that the hospital didn't have enough help to take care of them properly.

Among the group of men I had met were people from many walks of life—farmers, a plumber, a teacher, a minister, a coal miner, a rubber plant worker, and others. I had taken note of their religious denominations. Practically every denomination I could name was represented. They were here from every social and educational level in life, from homes of the poverty stricken, the middle class and the wealthy. There were those who could not write and others with college degrees. Among them were criminals, drug addicts, alcoholics and sexual deviants.

I felt as if I were accomplishing something. My presence on the ward had proven in itself a source of comfort to these troubled men. Many of them were afraid of this new, strange, frightening place in which they found themselves. Many were beset with feelings of guilt, fear, and loneliness. My presence had helped to form a contact with the familiar world of their past lives and everything that was normal. I helped to tie them to what they loved. My interaction with the men encouraged me.

I knew I had found my place—my ministry—and it was here, at Bryce Hospital.

-6-

It was good to be back in my office where I could review the experiences of the day. I felt tired but gratified. My thoughts went back to these mentally ill people. I had found most of them in a pitiful state of mind. They felt that life had defeated them. They were lost and dejected. They felt it useless ever again to make an effort to get out of the hospital. One man had said to me, "I've lost my citizenship and can't vote anymore." Another stated, "My folks don't want me. They say it would just be another mouth to feed and they can hardly get by on the small amount of money they now have to live on." Some felt they were too old. They had missed their chances in life. Their health was gone. Their dreams were already dead.

Yes, I thought, these people are in a pitiful state of mind.

I had seen the loneliness of these fellow human beings. It was appalling. Despite the crowding of dozens of people into a ward, their souls were so much alone. Their insulated lives were filled with fear, feelings of inferiority, feelings of failure, and the inability to get out of their own concerns and relate to other people. They needed so much to be accepted, to be liked, to be recognized for their true worth, and to be understood. Yet they

A depressed patient is comforted by a hospital attendant.

shrank from much-needed emotional contacts. They felt themselves prisoners of bolts and bars they could not break. The feeling of ache within them was tremendous.

I wondered about their backgrounds. Probably many of them had suffered some hurt or humiliation in childhood. Something, or someone, had destroyed their belief in themselves. They may have been mutilated by unkindness so that they had gone limping through life. Man was not meant to be a cringing being, eaten by anxiety, a prisoner in silent loneliness, living in blind cruelty. There is a soul sickness which needs to be considered and ministered to, else all other efforts to heal will prove only temporary. At times, it can outweigh any physical disorder. There is need for that peace with God which comes only through getting to know him personally.

Most of those who had come to the hospital had broken lives, broken spirits, or broken hearts. They needed more than censure or condemnation. Yet, in many cases, the family, the church, and the community had treated them like moral outcasts. They had ignored them heartlessly. This never heals anyone and can only make the condition worse.

In the following days I learned there were several reasons why families did not want their mentally ill relatives at home with them: (1) A feeling of being disgraced—they had a "crazy" person in their family. (2) Inability to cope with irrational, antisocial, or unpredictable behavior. (3) Economics—another mouth to feed. Possibly a patient who had been released from the hospital would not be productive in helping out with expenses. (4) Released patients frequently had difficulty fitting into society, both at home and in the community. The community was often afraid of the former patient, who felt the rejection. (5) Often, after patients had been released, their families continued to think of them as they had been before and did not credit the hospital and patient with attaining any improvement. The family assumed "once crazy, always crazy."

Here are all these people, sick and desolate, I thought. Why do people do the things they do? Why did that man molest his daughter? Why did this man choke his wife and beat her up? Yet I thought that some of them showed more sanity than some people I had known who had never been confined to a mental hospital.

My thoughts continued of these who seemed forsaken, forgotten and rejected by their families, by their churches and by society. These who were created by the same God who put breath into my own nostrils, these whose lives have temporarily become fouled up—why should they spend what seems like an eternity here? Why should they be treated as the offscourings of the earth? Why should people break all ties which had bound them together in a family?

Why, why, why, oh God? I thought. If there's anything I can do to help these people find the way to be released from their fear and guilt to faith and freedom, and gain confidence in themselves and security through you, show me the way.

I paced the room, pondering. Returning to my desk and sitting down, I reasoned that just as man has a physical and mental sense, he has also within him a spiritual sense. As I reflected on this, I was convinced that drugs, electric shock treatments, and all the other techniques of psychology and psychiatry could help people mentally and physically, but there remained a vast territory too little explored. Only an awakening of spiritual consciousness could help our patients become whole persons.

Therefore, I thought, it is not completely correct to speak of these people as "mental patients" whose needs are mental. They are also "spiritual patients," for their needs may be more spiritual than they are mental or physical. As long as we try to meet only their physical and mental needs, these people will continue to return again and again to the hospital. For some time yet they will depend on the physical and mental means of help. What is the remainder of the solution for the mentally ill, if not a better relationship with God? All the drugs, electric shock treatments, therapy from psychiatrists, psychologists, religionists, and recreational workers will not solve the problems of the so-called mentally ill persons unless the inner man is transformed—unless there is a change in his spirit. *Oh, God, help me to help these people.*

That evening at home, the phone rang. It was a minister friend calling. He began, "I read in the paper that you are now chaplain at our state hospital. Pardon my frankness, but it seems, Otis, that you are just throwing your life away. Why are you burying yourself with all those crazy people? You were meant for better things. What's got into you anyway? You will be just wasting your time and training there with the insane. What can you expect to do for them anyway?"

I replied, "You may be right. Maybe I am wasting my time and talents here but that's something I'll have to decide. Just give me time and I may be able to tell you why I've cast my lot with the mentally ill. I do not believe I am here as chaplain by any chance. I believe I was called to this work."

My friend continued, "You know, of course, that your work there will be a lonely one, a depressing one, filled with much hardship."

After our conversation, I pondered the words of my minister friend. Did he say I would be lonely in my work among the mentally ill? I asked myself. Lonely? I'll not be lonely because of my work, but lonely because there are so few with whom I can share my thoughts.

The faces of the men and women with whom I had worked that day came to my mind. I relaxed and tried to read the newspaper but their countenances seemed to appear on every page. Finally I put the paper down. I ate my evening meal but could not forget them. I spoke to Clytie Mae about it, saying, "I don't seem able to put those men and women at the hospital out of my mind. They seem to be right here with me, pleading with me and confiding in me, powerfully pressing in on my thoughts."

She handed me a letter. It was from a friend in another city, a man mature in the things of the spirit. I was anxious to hear from this old friend, who knew of my new work. The letter read:

> Dear Otis,
>
> I send you deep love. You surely are chosen for this work because of the great spiritual longing that you have—also your physical courage and love for Jesus. Yours is a great task, one which few would undertake. Never think it will overwhelm you, for many loved ones are helping you in prayer every hour of every day. Keep close to him, my brother, realizing your task will bring you much compassion of the heart. Be still; seek God; love Jesus and his sad humanity. Great is your work, but greater still is the love you will

draw to yourself from those you serve. You have undertaken a great task to take light to them that sit in darkness. Go forward unafraid in his service.

Laying the letter down thoughtfully, I was sincerely grateful for this communication. It was just the tonic needed at the moment. I knew God could have placed me in a life of greater comfort, but I already felt grateful that it was my place to serve the mentally ill.

There was another letter on the table waiting to be read. I opened it eagerly. It was from another friend who lived far away. It read: "Dear Otis, I am happy to hear of the wonderful opportunity provided for you to serve the mentally ill. God speed you on your way. I know his love will flow through you to those you serve." I smiled at the letter, recognizing God's affirmation. I needed only to accept his guidance.

I sat down at my desk to be alone with my thoughts. Resting in my chair, my mind went back to the patients. I couldn't get them out of my head. I saw them in despair and darkness, I saw them suffering and anguished, I saw them bitter and sorrowful. They were doubtful and fearful, dogged by remorse, without hope. As I thought about their misery, I felt a tremendous compassion and love for them. The doctors could treat their minds and bodies, but I knew that their spirits needed attention also. I wanted to enfold these dear souls in my arms to console them, to speak love and comfort to them. As I pondered this point, there came to me the realization that God does that very thing.

I had tried to let each patient I encountered talk enough to try to get the troubles out of his or her system. This was an important first step. I was willing to hear their stories. However, I determined that I did not want to waste time by letting them talk endlessly, repeating themselves. That would not be good for them. After they had talked awhile, I guided the conversation away from their frustrations and hopelessness. I tried to be cheerful and encouraging. I expressed confidence in them, hoping they would gain confidence in themselves. These mentally ill men and women seemed to have lost their way. I knew they were all created in God's spiritual likeness. No matter what their difficulties, I hoped that many of them would get well enough to go home.

I realized that in the days to come I must remember to keep my eye on my primary goal: to see that the patients at the hospital are led to a greater awareness of God's love. My convictions were so powerful that I almost spoke aloud: God is not the *last* resort in mental illness. He should be the *first*. The indwelling Spirit is indeed the power that heals and establishes peace of mind, tranquility of being. It comes down to one simple thought: As great as psychiatry is, God is greater.

I knew that in giving the highest and best within myself to the mentally ill, I would be fulfilling my calling. I needed only to let God express himself through me. I was at peace within myself and with the world.

Resting from my thoughts for a few moments, I rubbed my tired eyes and became aware of the lateness of the hour. I had been long lost in thought. I knew I must get a good night's rest and prepare myself for another day's work. I had heard of the "bull pen" and the dread that some of the fellows had for it, so I planned to visit it tomorrow and gain firsthand knowledge.

- 7 -

Turning my key in the door, I entered a large ward where a few men were engaged in general housekeeping tasks; they had chosen this work rather than going to the bull pen.* To make conversation, I stopped and spoke to a man who was sitting on the edge of his bed. "Are they good to you fellows here?" I asked.

"No, they are not," was the reply. "They sure do mistreat us. I'm a Baptist preacher. I try to read my Bible as I sit here on my bed. Those key men—those so-called ward attendants—come along and spit tobacco juice in my Bible." His Bible was open on the bed beside him. I leaned over and thumbed through

---

*Although the majority of patients were either unwilling or unable to spend any time doing work, many chose to be more active. The hospital buildings were located on a large tract of land, and some of the male patients farmed this land under supervision. There were a dairy and a peach orchard, chickens and hogs were raised, and mules were kept for plowing and hauling. The men who worked on the farm had their own living quarters in a separate building. Other male patients kept the grounds.

Female patients worked indoors in the laundry and with food services. Those who had clerical skills did typing and other office work.

These tasks provided relief from the monotony of the wards, and many patients eagerly sought work. Dr. Tarwater was often heard to say that work was one of the best possible therapies for mental illness.

several pages but saw no sign of tobacco juice stains. He continued with a hand on his throat. "Last night while I slept, they tied a rope around my neck and tried to choke me." I looked at the man's neck but could see no signs of mistreatment. I thought, The poor man must suffer terribly from delusions; to him these things are as real as though they actually happened.

I moved toward a patient who was mopping the floor and said, "My name is Thomas. I have come to be chaplain here." The man looked up with only casual interest. When asked how long he had been in this hospital, he answered, "Fifteen years." I asked him also, "Are they good to you fellows here?"

"No, they are not. They mistreat us awfully. The key men take some of us men out into the yard. They have no mercy. They tie us to a tree and whip us with a chain."

Both patients had spoken with such seriousness that a visitor in the hospital might well believe them, in view of the many rumors which have leaked out of mental hospitals about the treatment of people incarcerated there. I shook my head. Even I was asking myself, Are these men delusional or are they telling the truth? I decided I would wait and see. A large man with a crew haircut stepped up and asked, "Are you the chaplain?"

"Yes, I am. My name is Thomas."

"Well, I don't have any use for the preacher profession," he stated with feeling. "You allow things to go on here that shouldn't, and don't do anything about it. Let me give you an example. The people in the kitchen take good food and ruin it so it is not fit to eat. It's slop." He went on, "Then someone steals the things our folks send us. One of the patients had an epileptic spell in the bull pen. Those key men kicked him, then carried him to the disturbed ward. A lot of good that did him. He died. They put his body in a pine box and painted on it, 'Do not open. Died of infectious disease.' It was not infectious. They wanted it left closed because those key men killed that man."

I did not comment but, with a grave look on my face, turned to the ward attendant who had come out of his office.

THROUGH THESE EYES

I introduced myself but the employee merely stared at me coldly. He seemed to resent the presence of an outsider on the ward. "I don't see that we need any chaplain here," the attendant said bluntly. "It's a pointless job. You can't do these crazy people any good."

I did not appreciate the man's unkind remark, but tried to ignore the barb. In an effort to win him over, I said pleasantly, "Maybe I cannot help them, but I shall give it a try."

I moved to the door to the bull pen and stood there overlooking a huge yard enclosed by a nine-foot concrete wall. I saw a number of trees, most of which had shed their leaves; their October foliage was still evident on the ground. The yard was barren of any other vegetation. Masses of men milled about, walking aimlessly back and forth within the enclosure. Several lay asleep on benches or spread-eagled on the ground. Occasionally one could be seen reading a back-dated newspaper or a Bible or playing solitaire. Several domino and checker games were in progress.

As I observed this mass of human beings, I saw one man shadow boxing; another paced around a tree again and again in a well-beaten path which only he had travelled each day, almost to the point of exhaustion. Over to the side there was a man playing baseball. He would wind up and go through all the motions of pitching an imaginary ball. Still another elderly man, short in stature, whom everyone called Shorty, held a well-worn Bible in his hand as he exhorted everyone to "accept the Lord and be saved." His advice went unheeded. No one seemed to pay him any attention.

One man stood with his feet apart and jerked his body sideways, pushing against the ground with his right foot. His clenched fists and bent elbows contributed to the impression of forceful action. I asked an attendant what the patient was doing and was told that he was helping the sun to rise. He did this every morning.

There was a babble of meaningless sounds coming from the lips of some of the fellows as they talked to themselves. I felt there was also an undercurrent of fear, restlessness, and hopelessness. Over in a far corner near the fence, a thin little man was masturbating. Some of the men milling about nearby merely glanced in his direction and passed without a word.

As I gazed at all these wretched, unhappy, fragmented bits of humanity, the bull pen looked in some ways like a stockyard. In other ways it reminded me of the desperate pacing of lions in a zoo, the desperate pacing of creatures wanting to be free— free from what? Who could say? Was it to be free from locked doors and barred windows? Or free from haunting fears and guilt feelings?

Watching the several hundred men who once enjoyed the same freedom that was still mine, I thought, So this is the bull pen; what a place; what a life! I had never seen a sight so barren, so gloomy, so lifeless. I felt a chill just looking at it. As I stood there surveying the crowd, I asked God, Must I love these people? I don't know how to do it. Oh, I can *say* I love them but, truthfully, I just don't know how to love them. What am I going to do? I'm willing to be an avenue through which you, God, can love them. If that can be arranged, let's have it that way. Just don't ask me to love them on my own, because that is beyond my capacity. I cannot do it. God, you could love the thief on the cross and the woman taken in adultery. You love these people too. I know you do.

I decided to venture on out among the men. Several of them had noticed me standing in the doorway and moved in my direction. Probably more foolish than wise, I slowly locked the door behind me and walked down the steps to where a dozen or more men were standing. I felt uneasy as I looked around but the patients seemed friendly enough.

"Are you our chaplain?" asked the nearest man as he extended a friendly handshake. I looked at him in surprise.

"Yes, I am. My name is Thomas."

"Aren't you afraid to come out into this bull pen?" the patient inquired pleasantly.

An attendant locks a barrier between patient areas in Bryce's Main Building.

"Well, I'm not sure," I responded. "I have heard about the bull pen and I want to see what it is like, so I came out for a look."

"We don't like it," said another man, "but the key men make us come out here."

"Why don't you fellows like it out here?" I inquired, deciding to take a querulous tone. "It's a welcome change from being cooped up all day."

"It's too dangerous," he replied. "They have so many fights. You never know when someone will jump on you and beat you up."

I inched my way toward the center of the group while others at a distance came nearer. "I want to meet the chaplain," they would say. Soon I found myself shaking hands right and left. Some introduced themselves and I asked others their names. Eventually, I got to a heavy set, well-dressed, distinguished-looking man on the far side of the crowd. When I extended my hand and spoke to him he curled his lip and said, "You should have spoken to me first before you spoke to all those other fellows."

"Why is that, sir?" I asked.

"Because I am the prince of the world," he explained. "I have control over all the world. These men are all my subjects."

"What's your name?"

"I am Prince Edward," he replied.

"You know, sir, I am new here at the hospital and I'm trying to get acquainted with everyone. Nobody told me that you were the prince of the world. I will see you some more and we will get better acquainted."

I joined a small group of patients. Forgetting that I shouldn't display my ward keys, I held them in my hand. A patient came up behind me and held me tightly. Calling to the others he said, "Fellows, let's take the chaplain's keys."

"What is your name?" I asked over my shoulder.

"I'm Walter Vinson."

"Walter, you don't want my keys; you know you don't want to leave Bryce Hospital," I laughed, surprised at my own presence of mind. None of the other patients helped Walter. He laughed also and turned me loose. (I have been told that mental patients do not cooperate well with each other; this possibly explains the lack of response on the part of the other patients.) Disconcerted, Walter lay down on the ground on his back and did a trick for us: he took one foot and placed it behind his head, then did the same with the other. He didn't say anything and neither did anyone else. I moved away, leaving Walter to untangle himself.

A burly young man with a sullen and hostile look accosted me. "Who are you?"

"I am Chaplain Thomas."

"Chaplain, eh! What good is a chaplain here? What can a chaplain do to help us fellows in a place like this?" he asked sarcastically.

"Well, I am here to lend a helping hand in any way I can, especially with spiritual problems. I'd like to offer encouragement," I answered, unabashed, casting a glance around to the several men who stood by listening.

"Well, you can't help me, and I don't see that you can help anybody else. Pshaw! The very idea of a chaplain thinking he can do any good here," the fellow needled.

"Well, my friend," I said pleasantly, "it may be that I cannot help *you.*" With that I turned to another young man who wanted to speak to me. We sat down on a bench nearby. The man who had needled me came and sat cross-legged on the ground to listen.

In a calm, clear voice, the young man said, "Chaplain, my name is Barfield. I want to go home. They are not doing me any good here." Lowering his voice almost to a whisper, he said, "If I stay here, I'll go crazy like the rest of these people. They don't realize I don't belong here. There's nothing wrong with my mind. I want you to help me to get home."

"I do not know, Mr. Barfield, whether you belong here or not," I replied. "Someone must have thought you could get help or they would not have put you here. Of course, I know it's possible for them to have made a mistake. If you did need to come here, it is possible that you are now well enough to go home."

Barfield continued, "I haven't seen the doctor in six weeks. I work in the dining room, and he's too good to visit anyone there."

I remarked, "I'll be glad to see the doctor and ask him to consider your case." At this point, neither of us had any idea that this was precisely all that was needed and that the young man would be sent home in a few days.

Another patient spoke up, "I've been in a lot of places in my lifetime. But, chaplain, this is the worst place I've ever been in. They curse God. You can't talk to them. They talk good to you now and later will curse you behind your back. I can't do that. I'm a saved man. I'm 70 years old, and I aim to meet my wife in heaven."

He became emotional, wiping his eyes with his hand, then continued. "You know our world is in bad shape. I'm a veteran of World War II. I saved the world in that war and I'm working on this one. They sent two men from Washington, D.C., to get me to help them out. Some men have that gift and I'm one of them. If I get out of here, I'm going to save this country. Pray for me to get out so I can help them."

A small, bald man stepped forward. "I have no complaint with this place," he said. "Everyone is good to us here. If I needed to be here, I would not mind it, but I know I'm not crazy. I've been here eight years. It's time I was set free again."

"What would you do if you were out?" I asked.

"I'd get a job and make some money. I'd marry again. My old lady has divorced me since I've been here."

"You know it is not easy to get a job after one's been here as long as you have."

"I know that. But someone would hire me and I'd make enough to support me and a woman," the patient said confidently.

"You remember that house rent is high, so is furniture, food and clothing. Then you must consider utilities, which do not come cheaply either," I reminded him.

"Well, I am willing to try it," he said.

A slender young man in his thirties commented, "You know, chaplain, I love this place."

"Why?"

"You folks are so nice to us patients. It's just like that guy said. I agree. You understand us. The folks outside don't. You see, once we've been in here the people outside have given us up like we were dead. My wife divorced me too."

"Chaplain, I want to ask you a question," interjected a neatly dressed man who had come closer. "Do I talk crazy or do I make sense in what I am saying? If I'm crazy, I've always been crazy." He spoke seriously and waited for a reply.

"All you've said to me makes sense," I replied. "But you

know this hospital is for people who have many kinds of problems. Not everyone here is confused."

"Look at my hand. It's perfectly calm," said the man, holding his hand out as if to convince me he was not nervous either. Then he added, "I don't belong in here with all these crazy people. Really, I don't." As he spoke of "these crazy people," he had lowered his voice almost to a whisper, casting a hasty glance at his fellow men in the bull pen. "I'm just as sane as you or the doctor or anyone else," he added.

"I would not argue that point with you," I replied, "for I'm no doctor. A doctor and a probate judge had to sign your commitment papers before you could be brought here."

"I hadn't seen the judge until the deputy sheriff arrested me and put me in jail. They left me behind bars two weeks. My wife never even came down to see me."

"And the doctor?" I asked.

"He didn't examine me. I had never even seen him before."

"I think I understand how you feel about all of this," I said, laying a consoling hand on his shoulder.

"Well, I know this hospital is for the insane, but I'm not insane," he continued in a calm, but hurt voice. "If I needed to be here, I wouldn't mind it. But I don't belong here. I'm taking up a bed that a crazy man could be using. I want to go home. Call my people collect to come after me. They'll pay for the call."

"I'd like to help you, sir, in any way I can, but I'm not allowed to make calls. It's a rule of the hospital. The doctors don't make phone calls either, except in cases of emergency." The man shrugged and turned away.

"My name is Nelson, chaplain," a newcomer said, extending his hand. "Chaplain, I believe we've done something wrong and the Lord is punishing us for it."

"Mr. Nelson, what we often think of as God punishing us is really our punishing ourselves. Every man lives his own life and is rewarded by his own conduct. God never gives up on us."

THROUGH THESE EYES

Time passed rapidly. The men started filing toward the dining rooms for lunch. I rose from my seat to go with them and the burly young man who tried earlier to needle me also stood. "Chaplain, I want you to forgive me for talking like I did to you."

"Oh, I forgot about it already."

"No, you haven't," he said pleasantly. "Still, as I see it, they can let all the doctors go and replace them with men of God like you."

Another patient approached and said, "Chaplain, one of the men was going around saying you are nothing but a 'liquor head.' Was he telling it like it is?"

"What do you think?"

"I told him you were no such thing."

As I moved along with the men, I recalled that I had not seen even the semblance of a fight. I brought up the subject, whereupon one of the men said that two of the fellows had had a little fracas earlier in the day. He had gone to get the attendant to stop it. Finally the attendant was located sitting by the side of the building reading a newspaper. The men were angry with him, as they felt he should have been attending to his duties.

I watched some of the men as they filed into a dining room and took their places on long benches beside the tables stretching across the room. Food had already been placed on each plate. This was one of several dining rooms, each holding about 300 men. I passed along the aisles as they ate. Occasionally a fellow would look up from his food to extend a handshake. Others called me over to speak to them or ask me to pray that they could go home.

"Are you going to preach next Sunday for us?" asked one of the fellows.

"Yes, I will."

"What's the topic going to be?"

"I don't know yet. I haven't had much time to think about it."

"Why don't you preach on 'Perfect Poise in a Chaotic World'?" he asked.

"Well, that's certainly a timely and worthwhile subject, but I believe it's too big for me."

I moved on through the dining room, giving a gentle touch on the shoulder of one, smiling to another. Some did not respond, being too preoccupied with their own thoughts or too busy with their meal. As I reached the other end of the dining room, I heard some sort of scuffle and noticed an attendant hurrying. Sensing a disturbance, I looked and saw two men fighting. They had been seated side by side at their table and now were standing up. Each man had an arm locked around the other and a fist mashed against his opponent's nose. The attendant quieted them down, asked the cause of the trouble, and got them separated. They began eating again. I learned from the attendant that the men had been arguing about me. One had said that I really was the chaplain while the other had revived the rumor that I was just a liquor-head patient.

I returned to my office to relax for a while, and remembered the question the young man had asked me in the dining room: "What are you going to preach about Sunday?"

Suddenly I felt perplexed about this very thing. What could I say to these people that would really help them? Could I ever get over to them the fact that God is their refuge and strength, a help that is ever present in our trouble? Could I make them know God cares for them in their need, that God really loves them?

I received an inspiration: It is in God's plan for me that I am here. I will identify myself with the patients in every way at my disposal. They belong to me and I belong to them. I am here as a pastor, as a shepherd to lead them.

= 8 =

I left the hospital late on Saturday afternoon. In the hallway I met Dr. Rivers, who walked along with me.

"Well, chaplain, I guess you plan to give them hell Sunday."

"No, they've had enough of that."

"I guess you're right," answered the doctor.

I sat down at my desk at home that evening to prepare my message for Sunday morning. I reflected on the recent events, thinking of those I had met in the Ladies' Receiving Building and in the Men's Receiving Building as well as those I had met in the bull pen.

I knew that I had only seen a small part of the population. There came welling up within me a great compassion for these living, suffering, fellow creatures whom I would be facing on Sunday. I had no idea how many would be there to hear me.

It was now that I felt the full responsibility of my position as chaplain to the mentally ill. Sitting there, I pondered my doubts. What could I say that would touch the lives of those who would be waiting out there before me tomorrow?

My own belief was that many of the patients looked at Christianity and religion from a distorted point of view. It had been made negative, restrictive, and frustrating. I had to approach them properly. I thought to myself, If I am to help them, I cannot do it by means of human reasoning. Neither can I do it by criticizing their human faults. If I condemn them, that is no consolation.

I found myself totally engrossed in my thoughts of these people. I thought of Bill Kirksey. There was no use telling him he was an alcoholic. He already knew that too well. To remind him would not have been helpful.

My thoughts turned to a young prostitute and an older woman who had been living in adultery. It was not my business to condemn them. I knew something was eating at these people. Rather than criticize or condemn, I would try to tell them about God's love.

I did not see them, or anyone else, as "creatures of chance" or as "worms of the dust" who were at the mercy of a capricious deity. They all were children of a loving God. God created them in his image. It was simply that some had lost their way. Some were not well developed spiritually.

Brushing my graying hair out of my face, stretching my arms above my head and breathing deeply, I almost burst into speech. The only true religion is a religion of love—love for God and love for all mankind, I realized.

I scribbled a few notes which I thought I might be able to use. The thought came to me, It doesn't matter who these people are, where they are, or what their past lives have been. It doesn't matter if they may have made an emotional mess of their lives. The important fact is the love which God feels for them. He loves them as much as he loves me, for God is no respecter of persons.

My sincere desire was to help these people help themselves. I knew I could not help them by belittling them in any way. I recalled that in school a good teacher never belittles his pupil. Instead he appeals to self-respect. This appeal to self-respect is often lacking in many pulpits where preachers prefer to indulge in faultfinding. Jesus did not teach that we are offscourings of the earth, but the light of the world. He never belittled, but always sought to bring out the best in others.

A patient uses his hands to make jewelry and other craft items.

I thought further to myself, I must never put these people on the defensive by telling them they are sinners. To exhort them "You must do so and so" would only arouse a sense of guilt in my listeners. I must not point my finger at them saying, "You are bad people." It's not my job to accuse. I must include myself in my message and say *we*. The message must be directed to myself as much as to anyone out there listening.

I got to my feet, too stimulated by thought to sit still. I had to pace the floor. I must make it clear to these people that my place in the hospital is to help those seeking help. I must be careful not to encourage anyone to develop a dependence on me. I must help each one to find his own way, yet I must convince them I'll be there in case they need me. I sat back down. I believed those who were weak must have a longing, not merely for health, happiness, peace, or plenty, but for something deeper—an awareness of God's love for them. Then the thought came to me: I am well aware that as a human being I can do nothing for the mentally ill; Jesus told us that without him we can do nothing.

That settles it, I thought with a sense of victory within. If I am to help these people who are fearing hell, fearing God, tormented by sexual conflicts, and trying to run away from themselves, from life and from God—if I am to help them—I must first help them to realize that God's power is far greater than ours. With his help they can rise above their anguish, their fear, and their guilt.

Other questions came to me: How can I make the love of God more real to these struggling souls who have met with defeat? These will not be the well-adjusted whom I address, but miserable ones, lonely ones who are filled with terror and despair, abandoned ones and those who feel most forgotten.

How can I make the loving presence of God more real to these souls who are going through darkness and struggling for light and love and understanding? Will those who are sitting before me tomorrow see me only as another man experiencing the same problems in life that they have? Or, will they perceive me as a man called to bring them hope? My face was suddenly very grave indeed. I must trust God to take care of the worship service. Only then would my message be effective.

Lifting my head and looking up, I thought to myself, I will bring to these people only one message. It will be the truth of God's love. Then they must accept this on their own, not because of my ideas. I will present the truth and leave each one to accept what he or she is able to use. I will just let the love of God do its perfect work.

The hour was late as I stepped out into the night and stretched my arms toward the heavens. I was not aware until then of how tired I was.

–9–

Sunday morning came. I was to bring my first message to the mentally ill. A great sense of responsibility and a feeling of uneasiness possessed me. I wondered if all would go well.

At the appointed time I took my place on the platform. When I reached to open the large pulpit Bible before me, I found a piece of paper sticking out from under the cover. I knew I had not put it there myself. Opening the paper and giving it a hasty glance, I saw that it was a parody on the Twenty-third Psalm. It read: "The Lord is my shepherd. I shall not want. He maketh me to lie down in an insane asylum. He restoreth my soul. The key boys leadeth me to the table. They pour syrup on my hair. They lead me in every way but the right way. Yea, though I walk through the halls of an insane asylum, I fear lots of evil, for I have lost my common sense. The Lord have mercy on my soul."

Putting the paper in my pocket, I looked across the auditorium. I could not tell how many were there but I was informed later that there were approximately 600 people present. A large group of men and women had taken their places in the choir loft behind me. The pianist, Thelma Randolph, took her place on the piano stool. She was a college graduate with a degree in music and had played for almost all morning services and Sunday evening singings for several years. As she sat down in preparation for the service, she spoke, to no one in particular, "When Chaplain Thomas starts preaching, these folks will start having convulsions. When he begins throwing God and Christ at them, they won't be able to take it and it will knock them out." Occasionally a patient had been known to have a convulsion during worship services, and this probably prompted her remark.

I took my seat on the platform and looked into the faces of my congregation, seeing people who felt they were trapped in a mental institution, helpless to improve their lot. Their letters were censored. They were not permitted to use the telephone. They were not allowed to keep their own money, although few had any money to speak of. Many of them wore clothes furnished by the state. Here were hostile, resentful, desperate men and women, helpless fragments of humanity who were confused and disillusioned. Their faces portrayed their feelings as no words could. As I beheld this scene before me, I recalled the words of the minister friend who had told me, "You will be just wasting your time working with those people."

Looking more closely, I recognized Bill Kirksey, J. R. Gardner, and several others whom I had met. Yes, there was Prince Edward, the prince of the world. Then turning my eyes to the women's section, I saw Sharon, Sandra, Jo, Joleen, Mrs. Collin, Mrs. Norwood, and others whom I could call by name. Straining my eyes, I spotted Martha Richardson. She was a college graduate. The sudden change from a gracious household life into the cold world of a mental hospital was a difficult adjustment for this woman to make, as it had been for many others who had come this way.

Sharon leaned over and said to a neighbor in a whisper, "He must not be much of a preacher or he would not have come here to work with us. Probably no church would have him. Doesn't he know we are crazy? He can't do anything for me. I just came to church to get off of that ward." Her companion made no reply.

Next to the center aisle sat a pretty brunette who caught my attention when I saw a young man pass something across to her. Then I recognized the man as Buddy Allen and the woman as Mary Jo Barker. Was it Mary Jo's luck that her seat was directly across the aisle from Buddy? I wondered. I learned later that Buddy and Mary Jo had met at one of the weekly afternoon dances which were attended by the better-adjusted patients under nurses' supervision. As Buddy handed Mary Jo the note, he also gave her a big smile of approval which made her blush. She unfolded the piece of paper and a stick of chewing gum fell into her lap. She read:

Dear Mary Jo,

I'm feeling much better today. Just thinking about you all the time makes me feel better and, believe me, I think about you all the time when I'm awake, and even when I sleep, for last night I dreamed about you. I love you a lot because you are just who you are. I know I am the one to know when I am in love. For the first time in my life I am in love with someone, honestly and truly. It is the most wonderful feeling in the world. I don't quite know how to say it all. As soon as I met you at the dance the other day, I knew you were the one for me. I had never met anyone like you. I've never needed anyone like I need you. I need you more and more each day. There's no doubt as to my love for you. It is just a fact. Now won't you please let me know how you feel about me? Don't hurt me. If you don't love me, just say you love someone else and I'll quit speaking to you.

Buddy

Continuing to study my waiting audience, I thought of the maze of religious patterns represented here. There they were before me —27 religious denominations. There were differences in philosophy and emotion. How different it was from my former pastorates where there was a oneness of religious type and viewpoint. Yet everyone here had a need to be listening to the chaplain who might be able to help them.

There were those who had already sought my help, many sincerely, others only pretending religious belief. Some gloried in their meanness and in their ability to inflict hurt on others. Then there were the nuisances who hung on to you, sometimes whining or crying mock tears. Some pretended in silly or stupid ways to be very religious, or talked as if they were hopelessly lost and needing guidance like small children. Some were offensively loud in their conversation and possessive in their manner. There were those who lied, and those who stole from others on their wards, and those who cursed everything and everyone. Among them were alcoholics, prostitutes, and even rapists and murderers. Some ridiculed and mocked and sarcastically condemned all aspects of religion, including me. Some would probably leave the service with curses on their lips.

I stepped forward to announce the first song and the whisperings ceased and the audience became quiet. Suddenly I was surprised to notice a broad-shouldered man from the congregation coming up the aisle. The patient quietly stepped up to the platform where the choir and I were. At first I thought he was a tardy member of the choir, but before I knew what was happening, the man removed my spectacles with one hand and with the other hand struck me a violent blow on the cheek.

The congregation gasped.

It was like an electric shock to the entire assembled group. Two large men from the choir quickly stepped up behind my attacker to grab his arms if he attempted to strike me again. The patient, still holding my glasses, turned to the audience and said, "Folks, if we listen to this fellow, we are headed for trouble."

Then, without speaking to anyone in particular, he said, "Take me back to my ward."

Two attendants were already moving quietly toward us, their faces grim and determined. The patient started to give the spectacles back to me, then decided to place them instead upon the podium. Seeing the attendants, he nodded gravely and walked toward them. They escorted him from the auditorium.*

I had been so stung by the blow that I would have fallen had I not grasped the podium when I was struck. The lick left me dazed for a few moments. Then, recovering myself and without any reference to the incident, I announced a song. The congregation, obviously relieved, stood and sang quite lustily "O God, Our Help in Ages Past." As we sang, one of the men in the audience held his arm high and kept time to the music, as if he were directing the whole affair. A happy expression covered his face.

When the song ended, I opened my Bible to Jesus's words in Luke and read, "The Spirit of the Lord is upon me, because he hath anointed me to preach the gospel to the poor; he hath sent me to heal the brokenhearted, to preach deliverance to the captives, and recovering of sight to the blind, to set at liberty them that are bruised."**

I then took my seat and a choir member with a rich contralto voice sang "The Living Presence":

> *In the secret of His presence*
> *My soul has found repose*
> *And a voice within the silence*

---

* When I visited him three days later he apologized, saying, "I'm sorry for what happened. I thought you were a Communist." Mr. Stockton, the patient, came back to services regularly, and as long as he was at the hospital he would come up to me almost every Sunday to shake my hand and express appreciation for the sermon. He returned to his home about four months after my arrival.

** Luke 4:18, King James Version

Transmutes to joy my woes.
Here I lay my burden down
And deny the power of sin
For I'm conscious of the presence
Of the Christ who dwells within.

The soloist had sung in leading churches in her city and had held a responsible job in a major hotel. She became an alcoholic, although she denied this. Her brother committed her to the hospital and meant for her to stay there for life. Today she rose to the occasion and sang with a voice as beautiful as that of an angel.

When the song ended there was a great, expectant stillness. The place was charged with a spirit of receptiveness and I stood to speak. I knew in the hearts and minds of these people there was a great darkness, a darkness broken only by an instinctive knowledge that somewhere there must be some sort of God who cared. Before I began I prayed silently, Oh, God, I have no message of my own and of myself I can say nothing to these people. Have you a message for all these who wait before me? If so, speak, Lord, for your servant is waiting for you to speak through him.

Then I looked out at my people.

"Friends, it is no accident that you and I are here today. If only I could help you to understand that all the ages have gone before us to make up this moment, I would gladly do so." I used the tone I would use to speak to any of these people on a personal level.

"I do not preach sin and hellfire. That is not my business here. Rather, I shall try to tell you how loving God is. Maybe I won't sound like a preacher at all, as you know them, as I try to point to the law of divine love by which all should live. So long as I am your chaplain, I shall try to speak and live so that those of you who have ears to hear what I shall say may find the way to freedom within yourselves.

"You are here, my friends, not just to hear a man, but to fill your life with the love of God who can change your lives and release you from your fears, guilt feelings, and anything else that makes you miserable. We are here to seek the light, to get greater understanding of God and to learn what his eternal love can be. God loves you and me.

"In the journey of life we have to make many decisions. We have been given the freedom to choose the road we will travel. We have had this freedom from the beginning. If the road is rough and the going hard, let us not blame God. It is a road we ourselves have chosen to travel. Man chooses his own path. Sometimes we have only ourselves to blame when we bring disaster and sorrow upon ourselves. Let us be thankful as we gather here today that there is one who understands us, loves us, forgives us, and is able to deliver us from all our troubles. This brings us to our text of the morning, 'God is Love.'"

At this point I noticed that Buddy Allen shifted a little in his seat so as to be able to watch Mary Jo's face more closely. She smiled at him warmly before turning again to listen to the sermon.

"The words 'God' and 'love' mean different things to different people. With the wrong understanding of God, all life is interpreted wrongly," I explained. "To say 'God' is not enough, for men have believed in very bad gods. Most of us have looked into the kinds of mirrors which distort our appearance. They make fat people look lean and lean ones look fat. It is the same with our views of God; distorted pictures of him certainly are not the pictures Jesus gave us. Jesus said that God is a loving father."

I felt great compassion for my congregation as I continued.

"The greatest need of each of us is to know that God is loving, a loving father who is willing to lend a hand, to carry our burdens, and to help us get through difficult times. We think we have many problems, but our real problem is that we do not realize and accept the truth that God is love.

THROUGH THESE EYES

"The most powerful help for sickness or any other problem in life is a deep understanding that God is always present with us and loves every one of us. This can be a wonderful cure for many of our woes.

"It does not matter who we are, where we are, or what our past life has been; God loves us. He is not fickle or changeable in his love. He is the same yesterday, today and forever. His love never changes.

"God does not send trouble upon us," I explained. "He is willing to help us. He is not sending punishment upon us. God holds no ill will against us. He does not look upon any of us as incurably hopeless cases.

"Man often sees nothing more in God and his fellow man than he sees in himself. If he sees God as an angry, vengeful being, or as a vindictive, changeable being, then he really is seeing little more than himself—crafted as he is by his own ego and limitations. Such ideas are not in line with the life and teachings of Jesus, who tells us that God is love."

Behind me in the choir one of the women had written on her worship program, "I feel lost today 'cause you won't play hands with me." She handed it to the man who sat impassively beside her. He wrote underneath, "I have been warned by the attendants and patients that I would get in trouble if I did." He handed the paper back quietly. She wrote again, "I am not making any apologies to my family. My husband is probably too busy chasing other women and the liquor bottle to come to see me anyway." Her friend read this, then turned his thoughts back to the service. She did the same.

"God is the god of the brokenhearted and of those who are lonely and fearful," I continued. "He is the god of those who are bruised and afflicted in body, mind, and spirit. He is the god of those who are frustrated in their lives. God is the balm for every hurt in life. The greatest need in your life and mine, and of all the peoples of the world, is an awareness of our father and his wondrous love. Without this, the path seems tedious and unbearably long. Unless we can realize that God is with us as a living presence, we may feel that the future is hopeless."

Many were leaning forward in their seats as if anxious to catch every word as I continued: "I am sure there are many things which trouble you. There are the children back home. Who is caring for them? For some of you who have recently come here, there are business obligations which need to be taken care of; there are payments due on the car and numerous other debts; there is fear of losing your job. Yes, there seems no end to the things which drive peace from our lives. Will every day be as long as this? Will my life ever know peace and quiet again? Will I ever recover my former stability, or has even God forgotten me? We ask ourselves these and many other questions.

"My dear ones, whom God loves with an everlasting love, God is the answer to all our longings. For it is he who makes us complete. God is closer to us than hands and feet for each one who is ready and willing to accept him, if only we can or will open our souls to receive his eternal light, love, and power."

Buddy Allen and his beloved once again exchanged meaningful glances.

"God's love is here as it is everywhere. It is ours if we want it and even if we don't want it. Since God is everywhere, then he is as surely present here at this moment, as at any other place in the world."

At this point my message was interrupted by a feminine voice in the audience. She spoke clearly: "Chaplain, did I understand you to say God is here at this hospital?" All eyes in the house turned toward her.

"Yes, that's right."

"Well, I've just got one thing to say," she continued. "I sure do feel sorry for God."

There was laughter from the audience. It soon subside and she added, "I feel sorry for anyone who has to come to th place." More laughter erupted.

I continued, "Never before in your lives or mine has there

been so great a need for us to realize the presence of God. In our present time of need, it is God or nothing. For only God can help us to be complete. Nothing else. Only God can give us the peace our hearts long for. Only his healing love can bring solace to hearts that bleed, to minds that are confused and lives that are broken.

"Only God! Would that I could say these words so that you who are God's precious ones could grasp them totally and turn your whole beings completely to him, the father of everlasting and unlimited love. Perhaps you have tried other ways and failed. Turn now to the unfailing God. He is the surest answer to the problems of life. These, my dear friends, are not idle words. They are true words for today and for all days."

My message was complete. I knew from the prophet Isaiah that God's word would always be productive. I knew that no one, not even the mentally ill, can have God's truth presented to him or her and thereafter be the same as before its hearing. The truth might be rejected now, but its memory would survive and someday some of them would again consider the matter and investigate it further.

Once I had presented God's truth, I knew my hearers would never be able to get rid of it or lose it completely. I knew the patients' own intuition was constantly guiding them, and I hoped that eventually they would realize their Father's presence with them, expressing itself in their thoughts, words, and deeds. My task was trying to lead people from guilt awareness to God awareness. I knew this could be done, and when it is done a miracle is performed.

I asked for all the songbooks to be passed to the center aisle so the ushers could collect them. Buddy Allen, who happened to be one of the ushers, stepped across the aisle to get Mary Jo's songbook first, holding her hand just for a moment and giving it a gentle squeeze as he looked affectionately into her eyes and shared her smile.

A slender young man near the front stood up and, holding his hand cupped to his mouth, spoke loudly, "You've got to be saved, sanctified, and filled with the Holy Ghost."

Everyone looked in his direction, some with disapproval and others with pity for this outburst. Taking no notice of them, he repeated the cry. Two male attendants were moving quietly toward the man as he spoke a third time, still holding his hand cupped to his mouth, "You've got to be saved, sanctified, and filled with the Holy Ghost." Then, seeing the attendants, he sat down quietly of his own accord.

When all the songbooks had been brought to the front and deposited in their proper place, I signaled the end of the service and walked toward the door. The attendants counted the inmates one by one as they filed past them. Buddy and Mary Jo waved a farewell to each other.

I stationed myself by the door to speak with my congregation as they left.

-10-

"I'm sorry that man slapped you," remarked Mrs. Collin as the women filed out of the auditorium one by one. "He had no right to hit a nice man like you."

"Thank you," I replied. I smiled as the women came out first, to be followed by the men. Many ladies shook my hand and I tried to respond warmly.

Mrs. Norwood, who was waiting to speak to me, remarked to Anna Sanford, "The chaplain has an animated and resonant voice." She then turned to me. "You are so sincere. While you spoke, it gave my heart a lift—something I had great need of."

Anna Sanford remarked, "Chaplain, I'm not afraid when I hear you preach, as I am with my hometown preacher. He makes me feel I am condemned to hell and it frightens me."

Another woman who had heard her remarks said to me, "I am a church member. My name is Bessie Hall. The way my preacher preaches makes me afraid, but you're different; you give me hope. My preacher says we will go to hell if we drink cokes, smoke, dance, go in swimming, or watch television. He preaches against these things and says I will go to hell if I don't stop doing them. I've felt I was condemned to die, so I wanted to die 'cause I had done wrong."

I patted her hands lightly. "God wants his children to enjoy living and to be of service to others." As we spoke, several other women got impatient and passed on by, some smiling or patting my arm or shoulder.

Lynn edged closer. "You are such a holy man, I want to touch you." Sharon, who had come out of curiosity, passed by without speaking.

Joleen said, "I like the way you talk. My preacher gets up and just says a whole bunch of words. They have no meaning for me. When he gets through, I don't know what he has been talking about."

Martha Richardson, walking tall and erect, remarked, "That was the greatest message I've ever heard. It should have been recorded. After hearing it I feel so free inside."

"I'm glad you found it helpful," I thanked her.

Then came Sandra, smiling. "Your message sure did stir me. It made me want to be a different person."

Mary Jo approached and laid her hand on my shoulder. "Chaplain, I appreciate that message so much. I would love to place my cheek against yours." With that she leaned over until her cheek touched mine softly, then moved quietly on her way.

Patsy, a pretty, young brunette, said sweetly, "My husband told me to give you this." To my surprise she kissed me on the cheek.

Other women passed, some with a nod and a smile, others too occupied with their own thoughts to stop for even a second. Then came Mrs. Montgomery, whom I had visited earlier and found in a desperate state of mind. She had recently been divorced from a doctor.

"You helped me today with one of my problems. I've been holding resentment against my husband and my in-laws. I see now that is wrong. I want to thank you with a kiss for coming to us." And with that, she leaned over and planted a kiss on my cheek.

I was a bit embarrassed by these kisses as expressions of

thanks for my sermon, but I had already learned that anything can happen in a mental hospital. Certainly I could not refuse this expression and run the risk of offending these good people. However, to be paid off in kisses was a new experience.

Then there was Jean who said, "I loved your message today so much I, too, could kiss you for it, but I'm afraid they would give me a shock treatment."

The last lady said, "I'm sorry I coughed so much in church today. I sure hope it won't cause me to get an electric shock treatment. With the help of God, I will continue to miss those awful things." I assured her that her coughing would not cause her to get any shock treatments.

The men who had been waiting now moved toward me. Three fellows in wheelchairs were allowed to go first. As they had been waiting for the women to move on, one man who was pushing a wheelchair was heard to say, "I'm sorry that fellow hit the chaplain."

"I'm not," replied the man in the chair. "I'm glad he hit him, 'cause the chaplain's reaction showed us what kind of fellow he is."

As they moved on, an old man approached me and spoke in a confidential way, "Chaplain, if I'd been you, I would have knocked that fellow down."

To this I replied simply, "A man in his right mind would not have done what he did."

The fellow agreed, "No, I guess not."

Bill Kirksey said, "I'm sorry for what happened today. I don't see how you were able to go ahead with your message after what happened. That took great courage."

Buddy Allen asked, "Chaplain, why have you come to work with these crazy folks? Don't you know we are beyond help? Why didn't you stay out there where you could help folks?"

I answered, "Let's wait and see. Maybe I can help some. I believe I can or I would not have come to work here."

Several fellows passed on by, yet others waited to speak,

sometimes two or three extending their hands at the same time. The man who thought he was Prince Edward, prince of the world, held my hand and remarked, "You are a popular man around here. Anyone who is kind to us locked up here would be popular."

Another man drew nearer and spoke gravely, "I'm glad to meet you but I wish to God I'd never known you." Smiling, he asked, "Do you understand what I mean?"

"Yes, I believe I do."

"Yes, I wish I'd never seen this place," he explained.

Another man mumbled as he passed by, "This is no hospital. It's a hell hole."

"Chaplain, if God loves us like you said he does, why does he send us to hell?" a young man asked.

"No, my friend," I said. "God does not send anyone to hell. He doesn't want us to suffer. We choose our own paths."

Another man approached with a question about sin. "You told my girl friend, Lois, it was all right to cut her hair if she wanted to. You know what Paul says in I Corinthians about a woman's hair." Then with some feeling, he added, "I just don't care to hear you any more if you don't preach against sin."

I smiled and said, "Thank you, sir, for telling me." I did not recall having spoken to Lois about cutting her hair but decided not to press the matter.

Hearing a large, tanned man speak, I said, "My, but you have a strong voice."

He replied, "Well, I should have been a preacher instead of a nut."

"Why do you call yourself a nut?"

"Well, I'm in the nut house, ain't I?" he answered with a booming laugh.

"What of it?" I continued. "Going into a chicken house would not make you a chicken, would it?" He smiled and moved on.

A heavy man with a few days' growth of beard and bushy

eyebrows declined to shake hands. Instead he said, "You preachers just look at one side of a question. If you had a wife like
mine, you could not love her. Neither would you forgive her.
I'll die and go to hell before I'll forgive that woman."

A young man just behind him had heard the man's remarks.
Pointing with a twirl of his finger at his own head, he said, "He's
crazy in the head. Don't pay him any mind." Then he added,
"Chaplain, that was a damn good message you gave us."

J. R. Gardner spoke next. "You told us a lie today. I heard
it."

"What was it?"

"You said you were here to help us. Well, you ain't helped
anyone," he sneered.

"I've tried to."

"No, you ain't," Gardner replied defiantly while others
glared at him.

"I would like to help," I insisted.

"No, you don't," Gardner persisted. "You are just here draw-
ing the state's money."

An old man threw his arms around my neck, then looked
me in the face and said, "I love you."

I answered, "Thank you, sir, and I'm glad to know you."

Another patient was passing on by without speaking. The
old man looked at him and spoke angrily. "Aren't you going to
shake hands with the chaplain?"

"Hell, no!" he replied emphatically. "I'm not going to shake
hands with no damn preacher."

I reached out to another who said apologetically, "I guess
I'd better not. I have a venereal disease." I had been told that
on arrival at the hospital patients having venereal diseases were
treated; there was probably no cause for alarm.

"Did anyone tell you of the disturbance I caused the other
day when I refused to take a shock treatment?" asked another.

"No, they didn't."

"Well, I did," he continued. "Those shock treatments are

awful. I'd ten times rather be horsewhipped than take one. The first one seemed to help me but the last one knocked some screws loose in my head." While he talked others got impatient and passed on by. Someone patted me on the shoulder, then passed on.

One man showed me a printed paper. On it he had underscored these words: "Some states send smarter persons to their asylums than they elect to the legislature." I smiled understandingly. He folded the paper and moved on.

Another man said, "Chaplain, you don't know what it is to have your liberty taken away from you for 15 years. You carry keys and can go in and out of the hospital at will. You don't know what it's like to be deprived of these privileges."

"No, I don't know. It is no laughing matter to be locked up. God bless you." I smiled and gave the man's hand a strong squeeze.

A man in overalls and a blue shirt asked, "Chaplain, have you ever heard of anyone being treated like I've been treated?"

"How was that?"

"I was real sick in bed. The police came and got me. They said they were carrying me to the hospital but they lied to me and brought me here instead."

"Yes, I've heard of other people being treated that way," I answered.

About 300 men had passed by me on their way back to their wards. Some of them walked with their heads erect while others looked at the floor morosely. Some looked me squarely in the face while others shook hands without even looking up. Some, failing to shake hands, would whisper, "Chaplain Thomas," or tap me on the shoulder, while others completely ignored me. Some were well-groomed, wearing white shirts, ties, and suits of neatly pressed clothes; others had tobacco juice stains on their state-furnished garments. Some of the men smiled, while others had vacant expressions.

A man near the end of the line said pleasantly, "Well, chaplain, that message did very well, but it was nothing special, really; I've heard lots better ones."

Somewhat taken aback by this unexpected evaluation of my efforts, I remarked, "Sure enough?"

"You are damn right," the man boomed as he passed by.

A thin young man spoke. "I've been here at the hospital six years. I'm here 'cause I hated my daddy and wouldn't forgive him. I want to get more of that love you were talking about today."

Another young man had purposely waited near the end of the line so he might find more time to talk with me. He said in a desperate voice, "I must talk to you." I walked with him to a room on a nearby ward where we could speak with some degree of privacy.

The patient began, "I don't need shock treatments. I need God. I'm a sinner. I'm afraid." He dropped on both knees beside my chair. Clasping his hands to his chest, he prayed, "Oh, God, I'm an awful sinner. You've got to save me. I'm sorry for what I did. Help me, Lord. Help me. I'm on the ground. Help me so I can stand up."

Remaining there on his knees, he explained, "I heard a voice saying, 'I will cut off your left hand.' I heard the voice say, 'I'm going to destroy the world.' I'm not making this up to scare you. I'm not having dreams. I don't claim to be God, but God's coming right away. Nobody will believe me. They're going to burn in hell. I'm not trying to scare people. I'm just trying to tell people what God told me. God is inside me. He's telling me and I tell you. I don't claim to be God."

I listened quietly to this desperate, disillusioned soul. Soon, the young man rose to his feet saying, "I don't want to keep you longer. I've received strength. Thank you."

An elderly man who had attended the morning's service greeted me. "Chaplain, you are the answer to my prayers. I've been here 21 years. Twenty of those years I've been praying that God would send us a chaplain. You have your work cut out for you. Now that you're here, I will pray that God will bless your work among us and give you strength."

"Thank you, sir. I appreciate those words," I said sincerely.

An old man with a mustache and goatee, who had played baseball in the big leagues, said, "Chaplain, I want you to preach sometime on the hypotenuse of hypocrisy." I looked at him curiously, and he continued. "That's about the men who are monkeying with the moon. When they get back from the moon, they won't be any better off." As he started to leave, he asked, "By the way, are you going to the ball game this afternoon?"

"Is there a game?"

"Yes, it's the final game of the season."

"I'll be there." Perhaps this would give me still another chance to identify with the men.

Tired, I returned to my office to relax and be alone for a bit. As I reflected on the experiences of the morning, I thought, I can find no task more important than helping others find spiritual freedom and release from their feelings of guilt, fear, and frustration—helping humanity tread the spiritual path which leads one to God and the experience of his love.

It was time for the baseball game to begin and I had promised to be there. As I walked toward the field, men were coming from the west side and women from the east, taking their seats on the benches or standing around. Some of the players were already on the field warming up. Several of the patients had found a boyfriend or girlfriend at the hospital and were sitting with them watching the activity on the field. The hospital had a lemonade stand and I took a glass. I moved among the group, speaking with them, then took a seat on the bleachers.

Different ball teams in the city would come out to play against the Bryce Hospital team. The game began and was in full swing when a train passed the far side of the field on its regular run. John White was playing in the outfield for Bryce, near the iron fence separating the hospital grounds from the

Patients and staff members often compete in baseball.

railroad tracks. He threw down his glove and hurried toward the high fence, somehow managed to climb over it, and hopped on the train, which always moved slowly past the hospital area.

The authorities at the hospital telephoned the railroad station a few miles away and had a message sent to the train crew that one of the hospital's patients had boarded the train, and asking them to find him. John had always dressed neatly and looked like any other passenger. He joined the conductor in searching for a runaway mental patient. After some time the conductor realized that the man who was helping him was the wanted man, and John was returned to the hospital.

John White and I had been in the same graduating class at our high school in 1920. He had gone on to teach and I had gone my own way. I had not seen him for years when I encountered him at Bryce. He had been there 18 years and he was still there when I retired 14 years later.

On another occasion John told me he knew the exact population of every state in the United States. To prove it he went to his room and brought me a world almanac. Beginning with

Alabama, he went through all 48 states, giving the exact population for each state. Only once did he hesitate: on Kentucky he started, backed up, then gave the correct figure. I wondered why he had learned this information. Was he trying to prove his sanity?

Back in my office, I prepared to go home. Reaching into my pocket for a handkerchief, I found a note. I recalled that it had been given to me by Bill Kirksey. I read, "Chaplain Thomas, that Dr. Miller on the staff is a homosexual and SOB. He calls in the young men for interviews. He locks the door behind them, then he makes a proposition that if the fellow will do business with him, he will send him home sooner. I know because he tried me and J. R. Gardner and Buddy Allen. He is a menace and should be gotten rid of." I placed the note on my desk as I sat there, trying to decide whether to destroy it as the writing of a disillusioned mind or to give it to Dr. Tarwater. I decided on the latter.

Within a few days it was learned that Dr. Miller was no longer on the hospital staff.

-11-

"Chaplain, I've got to give some electric shock treatments. Would you like to come along with me today?" Dr. Rivers asked. Still new to the hospital and very curious about shock treatments, I readily agreed.

About a dozen ladies were brought into the treatment room, one at a time. Each one came in reluctantly, with her shoes off.

"Doc, do I have to take these shock treatments?" the first one asked.

Ignoring her question, he said, "Just climb up on the table."

The patient lay down on her back and a swab was placed in her mouth to keep her from biting her tongue. Several attendants and nurses placed their weight on her hands and feet and chest; otherwise, convulsions might jerk her joints out of place when the current was applied. Electrodes were placed on her head, a muscle relaxant was administered, and the doctor turned a switch. The patient's body convulsed, then became limp. Her breathing was hard, her eyes were blinking rapidly but glaring, and her face was flushed. The woman was removed from the table, placed on a cart, rolled into an adjoining room, and laid on a bed.

"How much electricity do you use?" I asked.

Dr. Rivers replied, "We usually use 120 volts of electricity for three-eighths of a second. The machine can be adjusted to various amounts."

By this time the attendants had brought in another lady. In a plaintive tone she said, "Doc, I don't want another shock treatment. Please don't make me take one." By this time she was on the table.

"Just lie down," was his only reply.

This scene was repeated with slight variations until all shock treatments had been given.*

"Does everyone who comes here get shock treatments?" I asked.

"No, there is some danger involved in giving a treatment. We do not give them without permission from the family. We only give them then to those who don't seem to respond otherwise. They used to be given to almost everyone. Now it is usually those who are depressed and not eating or talking, or those who are over-stimulated and inclined to talk too loudly or push others around," explained the doctor. "Let's go into my office, chaplain," he continued. "I have to interview a new patient."

When we were seated, he called, "Miss Kincaid, send Mattie Hackett in." When the patient had taken a chair, he closed the door, locking it.

"Mrs. Hackett, I just want to talk to you a little bit so we can get better acquainted. This is Chaplain Thomas who has come to work with us here."

"Chaplain, I'm glad to know you. I need your help while here. I'd appreciate it if you will pray for me, anyhow," said Mrs. Hackett. She was neat, strong, and prematurely gray. There were small bruises scattered on her arms.

"Mrs. Hackett, why did you have to come here?" asked the doctor.

---

* See footnote on electroconvulsive therapy or "shock treatment" on page 20.

"Oh, I got mad with my husband and blew my top," she replied.

As the doctor asked questions, he was busy writing her replies in his notebook, to be transferred later to Mrs. Hackett's case history. "Would you tell me more about it? Why did you get mad?"

"My husband is cashier of the bank at home. The auditors found $6,000 missing. An investigation was made and it was discovered my husband had taken it. It was in all the newspapers about it. I felt disgraced. I just couldn't take it. I blew my top."

"Mrs. Hackett, have you and your husband usually gotten along pretty well?" asked Dr. Rivers.

"No, we haven't," she answered. "He worked at the bank while I managed the store. We had a lot of arguments, especially about the way I ran the store. It was a source of constant friction between us."

"You have been here before, haven't you, Mrs. Hackett?"

"Yes, two times."

"I believe when you came here before, you said you were through with your husband."

"Yes, I did."

"Do you think you will go back to him this time?"

"No, I hope not. I feel as long as I live with my husband, I will keep having to come down here."

"Do you think the trouble your husband had about the money was what threw you off again?"

"Yes, very definitely," said Mrs. Hackett.

"How long have you been married?"

"Twenty-two years."

"You feel, except for the home situation, everything would be all right?"

"I think so."

After several other questions the interview ended.

During these early days at the hospital, I accompanied other doctors as well on their rounds. I spent a day with Dr. Morgan and the 900 men under his care. Even though this doctor took his work seriously and really wanted to help them, his task was so great that he had little time to spend with the men individually.

After the men got better acquainted with me, they would say, "We like Dr. Morgan, but he has so large an area to cover every day, he can only breeze through the wards. He doesn't have time to know us personally. How can he know when we're well enough to go home?"

As I followed the doctor on some wards, stale air, laden with a collection of repulsive odors, assailed my nostrils. Try as the attendants did, they could not get rid of the odors. A person staying on the wards got adjusted to the smell, but for one coming out of the fresh air, the stench was quite noticeable and sickening.

As we looked down one long, dark hallway, I saw men in all postures. Some were half dressed, a few naked and wandering up and down the ward, muttering to themselves. Some lay on the floor motionless, while others sat still, staring into space or with drooped heads and closed eyes.

In another part of the hospital, Dr. Sterling had responsibility for about 450 men, many of whom had just been transferred from the Men's Receiving Building to the main building. As I went with him, I noticed that he was the only doctor who found time to shake hands with all the men who came to him with their requests.

"Doc, when can I go home?"

"Dr. Sterling, I had a letter from my wife. She's sick and needs me there."

"Doc, I'd like to work in the Recreation Department."

"Doc, I'd like to work at the canteen. I won't run off. I promise you. I came in the front door and when I leave I want to go the same way."

"Dr. Sterling, I need to get back home. I just passed the civil service examination and have a good job lined up. If I stay much longer, I'll lose it."

"Doctor, I've got several installment payments coming due first of the month. My wife has no money. If I don't get back to my home and job, I'm going to lose my car, my television, and my deep freezer."

"Doc, will I lose my citizenship since I came here? Will I ever be able to vote again?"

"Dr. Sterling, I wish you would see if you can get my wife down here to talk to me. I love her and don't want her to get a divorce. I want to explain everything to her and save our marriage if I can."

"Doc, my wife is pregnant and we're expecting the baby any day now. We have three children at home. They need me. I wish you could arrange for me to go and be with them. If they ever needed me, they do now."

On and on went the barrage of questions and requests made of Dr. Sterling. He listened patiently, answered each one as best he could, trying never to make a reckless promise. He showed a genuine interest in each man's problem.

The day I went with Dr. Cutler, I found much the same situation on the women's wards as I had on Dr. Sterling's service. If there was a difference, it was that the women were more demanding. The problems were much the same, only viewed from a woman's perspective.

When I made rounds with Dr. Rolf and a nurse, he remarked, "All the women on my service are senile old ladies. It's rather a discouraging proposition. I have nothing to build on. There's no hope for any of them."

After the wards had been visited in rather a routine sort of way, we sat in his office chatting. Dr. Rolf remarked, "Chaplain, one day I was on a ward when one of the women grabbed my privates. She just held on and wouldn't turn loose. I've never had anything hurt like that did. Ever since then I've been afraid of these women and I don't go among them by myself."

My last assignment was with Dr. Alman. We went on the women's side of the hospital to back wards among untidy and extremely deteriorated women. As the doctor, a nurse, and I entered the untidy ward known as East 51, I was told there were over 100 women on this ward. This was the most disturbing sight of all I had seen. Although I had read about such things, I was not prepared for this. Three or four of the women were naked. A few wore faded cotton dresses, but most wore gowns— chemises— against their bare skin. Their hair was dishevelled. Almost everyone was barefooted.

Dr. Alman explained to me that every day was the same for these women: eat, urinate, defecate, then eat again. Walk the floor in idleness all day long or sit on a bench, or perhaps slump down on the floor of the big room behind a bench, or lie on the floor against the wall away from the others and try to sleep. There was nothing else to do. I was told that each woman got a bath at night and was given a clean gown to replace the one soiled with urine from sitting on the floor, or with blood from her menstrual period. The women slept in these gowns and wore them the next day until time to bathe again. Before the day was over, some would take off the gowns and refuse to wear them. Others would tear theirs partially off.

After several weeks my informal period of orientation ended, from admission buildings all the way to the back wards. During this time I had made rounds with all the doctors on almost a hundred wards. I sat down to reflect on what my eyes had beheld. I had asked few questions; there was already more than I could grasp. The questions would come later. I remembered the ugly walls, dark gray throughout most of the hospital, except where the plaster had fallen off and been replaced with a rough patch of lighter gray. There were no pictures on the walls and no curtains at the windows. Dark brown benches lined the walls. All the wards looked much alike, bleak and barren. A peculiar stench like none I had ever known had penetrated my nostrils on several of the wards.

I reflected on the insufficient number of doctors and nurses, the shortage of attendants. How could they give the needed care? Many of the aides here were poorly trained, overworked, discouraged.

Most of all, I reflected on the thousands of men and women whose lives were wasting away, most of them in idleness. It seemed that all the faces of men and women, young and old, were alike. Everyone seemed to have the same expression of despair and hopelessness in his or her eyes. It seemed just a mass of humanity wasting away, with no end to it all. I had heard one pray, "Oh, God, I'd rather be dead than this." But death would not come.

I asked myself, How can I ever make an impression upon these unfortunate, pitiful human beings, who are often neglected by relatives and, in some measure, by the state? How can I ever bring the light and love of God to these darkened lives? I remembered my friend's remark: "A preacher is just wasting his time away working in Bryce Hospital." Maybe he was right after all.

But even with unsightly wards, falling plaster, fire hazards, ugly toilets and too few of them, poorly trained personnel, a shortage of doctors, inadequate and crowded buildings, I had observed several shafts of light illuminating the darkness in Bryce Hospital. Over against all the ugliness, foul-smelling wards, and insufficiencies, I had seen much good work being done. I had met many fine people at Bryce—doctors, nurses, attendants, and supervisors—who manifested a genuine interest in those for whom they were responsible. They seemed to be doing excellent work against impossible odds.

-12-

After several weeks at the hospital I sat at my desk and recalled Dr. Tarwater's words: "We have never had a chaplain, so you will have some pioneer work to do." That very morning he had asked me, "Would you like to go to Columbia, South Carolina, for a 12-day training program at the mental hospital there? You might find it helpful."

"Yes, I think I'd like to go."

"The state will pay your expenses. You'll need to leave right away."

I left the next day, but even so I missed the first day of the program. I was surprised to find only one other person attending, a chaplain from Tennessee. Our training was very unstructured. We accompanied the hospital's chaplain on his rounds of the wards and assisted him with worship services. Although I was there for 11 days, nearly everything that was taught was what I had already been doing at Bryce. The most positive thing about the time spent there was that it helped me realize that I was on the right track, at least by the standards of the 1950's.

Early on I had jotted down a few things which I felt were a needed part of my chaplaincy program. I knew that I had touched the lives of quite a few patients; however, these were only a small part of the 4,500 or more persons for whom the state was responsible. Here was a segment of our society the public barely knew existed and for whom they had little concern. All my life I, too, had been one of these unconcerned people.

However, there was one concerned group: the relatives of the patients. Yet they usually felt embarrassed or disgraced, and many of them tried to keep secret the fact that they had a relative in Bryce. If they dared to discuss the matter they would often say, "I don't know how he (or she) got that way; we have never had any insanity in our family."

I would continue to visit new patients as soon as possible after their arrival and write letters to their families. In these letters I would try to assure them that mental illness is no more a disgrace than physical illness and that many of the mentally ill get well and return to their homes and loved ones.

I had already established a regular day to visit the disturbed ward in the Ladies' Receiving Building for devotional services (which were well received). I decided to see what good could be done through music and group singing. I planned regular services on several more wards, about ten services in all, some weekly, others monthly.

Securing a portable record player and several of Tennessee Ernie Ford's records of familiar sing-along songs, I began my activities. It gave me another way to let the patients know we cared about them, and many were responsive. The ward attendants were cooperative for the most part. They would say to the patients, "The chaplain will be here for devotional services. Let's get on a clean dress and comb your hair." I would move along among the patients, shaking hands with them, saying how neat they looked, and thanking the attendants for their cooperation. We all sang along with the records, I made a few remarks, read a brief scripture about God's love for them, and said a prayer.

It didn't always go this well. One day I visited one of the

back wards where the most hopeless patients lived. This was a women's ward for about 40 patients. I went without my record player, not knowing exactly how I'd be received. As I entered, I found the attendant mopping urine and feces from the floor, for these people did not control their bodily functions. I tried to speak some encouraging words to the lady who was mopping. As I looked over the group of women it seemed that everyone was talking to herself or chattering meaningless words. No one seemed to be listening to anyone else; some were louder than others.

I began a familiar religious song, a verse of "Blessed Assurance," then "What a Friend We Have in Jesus." Before I had finished the songs most of the ladies had stopped their chattering and were listening. The songs had a quietening effect on all except one lady who was standing in a corner facing the wall. She continued talking although the others were attentive to my voice. I quoted the Twenty-third Psalm, feeling the women would recognize it. No one joined me.

I never went back to this ward. My experience there was very difficult for me. I felt awkward, uncomfortable, and out of place. Looking back, I wish I had persevered.

Soon afterward, I visited one of the men's back wards. In this ward some of the patients persistently tried to tear off all their clothes. Because of this they were put in coveralls with long sleeves that covered their hands; the sleeve ends were tied securely so the men couldn't unfasten their garments. This time I took my record player and the Tennessee Ernie Ford records. As the music played I moved among the group, extending my hand to those whose hands were free. No one shook hands with me or responded in any other way. I did return to this ward several more times and gradually, on these later visits, some of the men voluntarily drew nearer to me and the music. I continued to initiate shaking hands and over time some of them responded.

I didn't carry my experiment with music as far as I might

Under the direction of Associate Chaplain B. W. Allen, at left, the Bryce Hospital Touring Choir presented concerts across Alabama for more that 20 years.

have. The pressure of time caught up with me as my duties expanded and I couldn't do all the things I wanted to do.

Among other things, I visualized the time when we could have a choir director to train the chorus. We could make tours to communities where we had been invited and present programs at churches. This would help overcome some of the public misunderstanding regarding the mentally ill. Eventually this came to pass.

The Reverend B. W. Allen joined the staff on a part-time basis as an associate chaplain with responsibility for our choir. He had a wonderful gift for this work; the choir sang their hearts out for him. The hospital administrator was very supportive of the music program and provided a bus for the choir's trips to churches. These concerts were quite in demand, and for their part the host churches welcomed our singers with warmth and kindness. It was common after a performance for the church to have a fellowship meal, seating patients and members side by side so that they could visit with each other.

I was responsible for all tours within the hospital. The group might be any size, from one or two people to large groups from high schools or colleges. We were glad people wanted to see the hospital so that they would get a better understanding of the care and treatment given to mentally ill people here. I gave the visitors some orientation before going through the wards and then an opportunity to ask questions at the close of the tour.

Interesting or amusing things occasionally happened on these tours. On one ward there was a woman who carried a Bible in her hand and wore a shifty eyed expression on her face. "Whoremongers. Whoremongers. Whoremongers," she muttered as she wandered about her ward. One day I paused so that some lagging tour members could catch up with the rest of the group. Before I knew what happened, this lady had planted a kiss on my cheek. After the tour, the attendant who had locked the door behind the group approached me.

"That woman kissed me," he said. "Why does it always have to be the ugly ones?"

"I know. She kissed me, too."

On another ward of about 40 elderly men there was a dignified, well-groomed, portly gentleman who was very friendly. He often stood by the window looking out at the trees, sky, and clouds. I frequently took tours through his ward and when he saw me he would walk along beside me, making some remarks, looking at me, and chuckling to himself. An attendant told me that this man believed he was God and had made the world; he liked to look out the window at his handiwork. The patient never told me directly that he was God. However, on one tour as we walked along, he put his hand on my shoulder and said, "You are one of my mistakes."

On another occasion, as I walked with an elderly woman on a disturbed ward, a teenage female patient slipped up behind me, snatched my glasses from my face and threw them down, breaking them. However, violence against my person was an extremely rare occurrence. On the contrary, the patients nearly always exhibited courtesy toward me. I had gone to Bryce as frightened as a scared rabbit and was both relieved and pleased to learn that my charges respected me as their chaplain and treated me accordingly.

One outstanding exception to this was an experience with J. R. Gardner. On a visit to the criminal ward where fewer than a dozen men were housed, I recognized J. R., whom I had met soon after his arrival in the Men's Receiving Building. I recalled that when J. R. was born, his unwed mother did not want him. His grandmother took care of him until she could no longer manage him, then placed him in an orphanage. He was later sent to the boys' reform school and from there he was transferred to Partlow State School for the Retarded. From there he was sent to Bryce Hospital.

When I greeted J. R., he asked me for a cold drink and I gave him a dime to buy a Coke. Other patients asked for dimes also. I had several in my pocket and gave them all away.

Soon afterwards at a staff meeting a doctor reported that J. R. had escaped from the hospital. "He hid behind the door to his room and then called for a guard. The man went to the room, not suspecting anything. J. R. had a broken Coke bottle. He stood behind the guard, wrapped his arms around him, and demanded the man's keys—or else J. R. would stick the broken glass in his belly. The guard gave J. R. the keys and he made his escape." It was rumored that J. R. was hiding in the magnolia trees on the hospital grounds and was carrying a pistol. I felt guilty when I heard this news, wondering if one of the dimes I had given the men had bought the Coke bottle J. R. used to threaten the guard.

Every Sunday evening all patients who were sufficiently well-behaved, and who wanted to do so, came to the auditorium for an evening program. Every three months we had a communion service, but all other Sunday evenings we had singing, with me in charge. I felt that singing religious songs could have therapeutic value. Since I wasn't much of a song leader, I would select one of the patients to lead the singing. One of the ladies was a particularly good piano accompanist and often some local quartet or church group would come and sing for us.

On the Sunday evening after J. R.'s escape I left the service and began walking home along doctor's row, the long drive leading to the hospital. My car was temporarily out of commission, and I planned to catch the bus when I got off the hospital grounds. The moon was just rising and cast its light for me to see my way. With my mind on the good singing of the evening, my thoughts were suddenly interrupted by a low voice. "Hey, buddy! Wait a minute." Unsuspecting, I waited. As the person drew nearer I recognized J. R.

"J. R., what are you doing here? What do you want?"

"I want two dollars."

I realized it was a holdup and looked up and down the street for a car or someone to help. A light was burning on one of the doctor's porches, but not a person was in sight.

"Don't you run," J. R. cautioned. Remembering that he was suspected of having a gun, I decided right quickly that I wouldn't run.

"Why do you want me to give you two dollars, J. R.?"

"Because of the way you've treated me."

"J. R., I do not remember ever having mistreated you. You know I gave you a dime for a Coke?"

"I want three dollars," he said, raising his voice and the amount. No car had come along and I decided I had better give J. R. three dollars. I took out my wallet, and as I reached for the bills he suddenly grabbed the wallet with one hand and with the other shoved me in the chest. I reeled backward and fell to the ground. J. R. fled into a nearby cornfield. I got up and looked for my wallet. I found it in the dirt, empty. J. R. had taken all my cash, about $30.

I ran to the nearest doctor's house and told him what had happened. He phoned the hospital. Someone suggested calling for bloodhounds but this was overruled. A night guard came and carried me home, assuring me that I had done the right thing. I had not felt scared during the episode, but when I got home and began to tell my wife the story, I started to tremble all over as I began to realize what might have happened. Surprisingly, however, I easily went to sleep later on.

About one in the morning the phone rang. "This is the police department," a voice said. "We think we have your man. Could you come down and identify him?"

At the station I greeted J. R. "Hello, J. R." To the policeman I said, "Yes, that's the man."

"Here's the rest of your money, chaplain. Twenty-six dollars." I was told that J. R. had paid a man on the street to go into a store and buy him a sandwich and a package of cigarettes. The man's suspicions were aroused and he called the police.

The following day Dr. Tarwater asked me to come to his office. "Chaplain, we have J. R. What do you want us to do with him?" Without a moment's hesitation I replied that I didn't want to see J. R. anymore.

I have often wondered what happened to this young man who was unwanted by his mother, his grandmother, the orphanage and the reform school; was too difficult for Partlow to handle; and was unwanted by his chaplain and a problem for society. What could be worse for a newborn baby, or child, or anyone than to be unwanted?

-13-

I entered the disturbed ward of the Ladies' Receiving Building and walked down the hall, overtaking two old ladies who were talking with each other.

"Old woman, you haven't got a bit of sense." I recognized the speaker as Mrs. Norwood.

"Yes, I have got sense, too," her companion replied calmly.

"No, you haven't. You are crazy. If you weren't crazy, you wouldn't be here."

Mrs. Norwood's companion turned and walked away without a word.

"Good morning," I said.

"Chaplain, we are all as crazy as we can be. Look at her," she said, pointing her finger at the retreating figure. "Did you see the way she drools saliva? You know she's crazy. It's like a mad dog; it's a sure sign."

I unlocked the screen door between the ward and a sitting room. As we entered, Mrs. Norwood continued, "I'm crazy. I know I am. I didn't think so when I came here, but since being around these folks," she waved her hand at the other ladies around us, "I now know I am."

"Well, I know I'm crazy, but Dr. Rivers is crazy, too." The

speaker was Lynn, who had kissed me on my first visit to the ward. "He's crazy in a normal way and I'm crazy in an abnormal way. Can I say just what I think he is?"

"Yes," I answered.

"I think he's a son of a bitch," Lynn stated with feeling.

"Oh, Lynn, you shouldn't talk like that," Mrs. Norwood chided.

"Why do you think that?" I asked Lynn.

"'Cause I'm afraid he's going to give me shock treatments."

"He only gives them if your family gives written permission and if he thinks they'll help you get well," I tried to console her.

Smiling through blue eyes, Margaret, who had been standing nearby, spoke. "I know now that I've been crazy. They tell me I've been here three months. I didn't know where I was until this morning. It puzzles me. I don't know why I'm here. Did I do something awful?"

"Oh, I suppose not," I said. "Your home doctor probably felt you needed help and sent you here."

An elderly patient joined our conversation. "Our doctor here is crazy. He ought to be locked up here instead of us patients. I've got arthritis and they won't even give me an aspirin for it. Would it break the hospital just to give me an aspirin? Are they that poor? I brought $5 worth of medicine for arthritis when I came here. They won't let me have any of it. If I ask for an aspirin the nurse says she is going to lock me up. This doctor is crazy. I have a doctor back home. He's got sense!"

I listened patiently as she explained her plight, knowing that she would feel better just to have someone listen. She moved away to a chair and a patient I didn't recognize joined us.

"Who is he?" the newcomer said to Lynn. "He seems awfully nice."

"He's Chaplain Thomas. He is nice," said Lynn. "We're all crazy about him. Chaplain, I want you to meet a new lady. This is Susan Foster. She's been here about a week."

I grasped Susan's extended hand and she said, "You must not be much of a preacher or you wouldn't come here to work with us. Don't you know we're crazy?" She laughed lightly.

"Who said you were crazy?" I returned her smile.

"I asked to come up here. I'm one of the few who did. I made a grave mistake. Could I talk with you privately?"

I nodded, excused myself to the other ladies, and led Susan to a small room where I often visited with patients in private.

"I respect you," Susan began, "but I don't believe in your God." She had large brown eyes and her dark hair flowed loosely down her back. "Chaplain, this is no place for me. I don't belong here. I'm not crazy. Honest! My mind is as good as it ever was. If I'm crazy, then I've been crazy all my life."

She paused before continuing. "I tried to kill myself and asked to come here. The doctor saw me for about five minutes to give me a physical. I asked for an aspirin for my headache and he just laughed and moved on. He's not going to help me. They've got too many more worse than I am. Why did he accept me? This place is understaffed."

Susan's distraught eyes sought mine as she shifted slightly in her chair.

"After you try so hard to get help and they don't help you, you finally get discouraged and give up. They aren't going to get any cooperation out of me from here on. If they get anything out of me they'll have to pick it out of me with pick and shovel. I don't care whether I eat or sleep or do anything. I see I made a bad mistake coming here."

Susan's hands rested carelessly in her lap as she continued. "I don't have confidence in anyone. My granddaddy died of cancer. I wanted children but God wouldn't give me even one. That's why I don't believe in God. I don't have any faith in God and I don't pray."

I knew this confused woman needed help, but I also sensed it was time to end my visit with her. I rose to my feet and Susan did so also, clasping my hand in hers.

"Even though I don't believe in God and prayer, chaplain, I know you do. Pray for me. If I stay here much longer I'll lose every ounce of sense I've got."

"Of course I'll pray. God *can* help you."

We returned to the ward and Agnes approached me. "How are you?" I asked.

"Oh, I'm insanely happy," she answered. "I may be crazy, but I'm having a lot of fun being crazy." She suddenly became serious. "May I talk privately with you?"

We found a quiet place and she began. "Dr. Rivers can't help me. I'm happy being myself and I don't want to change. All he's got to do is call my mother and tell her he can't help me and for her to come after me." She paused briefly before asking, "Do you think I'm crazy?" Then, without waiting for a reply, she hurried on, "I'm happy being me. Call it hardheadedness or whatever you will. I don't want any help. I don't want to change when I'm already happy with myself.

Agnes was a pretty and slender brunette in her late teens. I was aware of her recent attempt to run away from the hospital. She had climbed a wire fence enclosing the yard where patients went for fresh air and sunshine. Several attendants had given chase. Agnes asked two men sitting in a nearby car to help her escape. They refused and she ran again, trying to elude the attendants.

She reached two men in a truck and begged them to help her. They agreed and were helping her into the truck when the attendants, six or more, caught up with Agnes and pulled her away. They carried her, kicking and biting them, back to her ward. This was the picture that flashed through my mind as Agnes repeated, "I'm happy with myself just as I am. I just want to be left alone."

She continued speaking calmly and pleasantly as I listened. She often looked directly into my eyes, and sometimes a faint smile broke out on her face. "Maybe later I'll want help, but not now. If I stay here until doomsday, I won't change. I can be just as stubborn as that Dr. Rivers.

"I'm not nervous. See!" she said as she held out her hand to me. "I'm not angry with the attendants for bringing me back when I ran away. They were doing their duty. I'm not going to cry. I'm just going to live up the $3 a day that the state pays for my keep. That's all I can do. It's up to that doctor!" I rose to go and she smiled at me. "Thank you for listening to me."

"And how are you today?" I asked Anna, a young divorcee in her late twenties.

"I'm stupid," she answered without hesitation. She seemed ready to talk so I sat down beside her. "My folks said I was stupid and that's why they were putting me here. If I am, then I've always been stupid." She tried to be pleasant to me, but there was resentment in her voice. "I'm no more crazy than the man in the moon. My folks really think I'm crazy, but I know I'm not. I've got more sense than I ever had. In fact, I've got so much sense I don't know what to do with it."

She laughed a silly laugh.

"I may be in the crazy house, but I've got plenty of sense. I can read between the lines." She paused briefly. "It's the funniest thing. Our folks put us here in the crazy house and then the nurses and attendants expect us to act sensible. If we don't, they punish us by locking us up in a room."

"Anna, that is not intended for punishment. Sometimes we just need to get away from the crowd."

"Oh, yes, it is to punish us," she replied. Then she went on, "You know, my folks came to see me. I told them if they thought I was crazy, I would keep that doctor guessing. I would act manic-depressive one day, paranoid the next day, and catatonic the next." Laughingly she added, "My ex-husband was a doctor. He told me how they act."

We started to part and she said, "Sometimes I feel like I could scream, but if you cry or stump your toe, they think you're crazy, and I'm sure not crazy." She raised her arms above her head, and with clinched fists and a frown on her face, addressed a woman next to her. "If I'm not already crazy, I will be soon if I stay on this ward much longer."

An old woman walked slowly toward me. Taking my hand to steady herself, she began talking. "I'm a widow woman, 75 years old. All I've got is my home. I have no business here. I was railroaded here. That sheriff who brought me here said someone told him to bring me here. When I see him again, I'll give him a piece of my mind. My sister did this to me. She is meaner than a snake in the grass. I'm as sane as any person in the world. I'm not crazy, I tell you," she said, shaking her head, her voice weak and trembling.

I spotted a vacant seat and led her to it. She sat down and, still holding my hand, continued, "I don't belong here. The family of Davis that I belong to don't go crazy. I don't come from that kind of family. If I were crazy, I'd know it. I've got no more business being here than in Jericho. I've got no business here.

"My husband died four years ago. I lived alone. A woman was tearing pillars out from under my house. They brought me here 'cause I tried to get the sheriff to arrest her. She's been doing this for 16 months. She would tear a pillar out, then dig a hole and put it in the hole and cover it up. Then she would haul it away. They said I was crazy, but I could see it with my own eyes. I'm going to tell the truth, even if they did put me in this place."

I smiled at her, "I'll be back to see you again soon and we'll talk some more." She smiled back at me and slowly released her grip on my hand.

Another patient motioned me to her. She was young, buxom, and pretty. "This is a devil's den," she began. "The hospital and you all are nice. But these other people—my god!" Putting her hands to her temples, she shook her head as if to shut out the thought of it all. "Yes, this is a devil's den. These people would drive one crazy. I'm sane." Pointing to her head, she added pleasantly, "There's nothing wrong with my mind. I've got to get out of here before I go crazy. You put a dog in a cage and he'll go mad if you don't give him a shot. They're giving me shots and pills and they're making me sick. The things we see and hear on this ward are enough to make one crazy. Chaplain, I want out of here. This noise, fighting, and cursing are getting on my nerves."

"I'm on this ward three times a week," I said. "Seldom do I hear any cursing and I never see any fighting."

"Well, they do when you aren't here. If I don't get out of here I'm going to be crazy as a loon."

"I will, too," interjected Mildred, who had been listening to the conversation.

"If there's any bit of a Christian in you," spoke a new voice in tones of desperation, "you'll let me out of here to go home to my people."

"Mrs. . . .?"

"Duncan." She supplied the name.

"Mrs. Duncan, arranging for you to go home is the responsibility of the doctor."

"Why don't you pray to die and go to heaven and get out of all this mess?" Mildred asked her.

Mrs. Duncan was a tall, thin, young woman with a swarthy complexion. Ignoring Mildred's question, she continued, "This place just doesn't agree with me. They fight, they scream and holler at night. They beat and pound on the door so one can't sleep. I didn't sleep a wink last night. If I stay here much longer, I'll be crazier than I was when I came. I don't like this place. *Really*, chaplain, what can I do?"

"The more you're able to cooperate with the hospital rules and regulations, the sooner you'll be moved to a quieter ward."

"Thank you! Thank you!" she said, squeezing my hand firmly and smiling.

Turning to a large woman, I asked, "How are you today?"

"I'm half crazy," she replied simply.

"Who said so?" I asked.

THROUGH THESE EYES

"I know I'm half crazy. I don't have more than half my mind."

I approached a young woman who was crying, and put my hand on her shoulder. She looked up. "Chaplain, I'm as crazy as hell." Then, realizing what she had said, she apologized. "Pardon me, I didn't mean to say that to you, but I'm confused. I'm as confused as the man who dropped his chewing gum in the chicken yard." She smiled a silly smile, then continued. "I didn't come here 'cause I was crazy. I'm just nervous. I took a course in Bible prophecy. That ran me almost crazy. It said we would be bombed in 1972 by the Germans and that all those left would be taken in slavery."

Another patient interrupted, "I was on my way to a Mother's Day church service when they got me and brought me here. There's nothing wrong with my mind. 'Cause I believe in God, they say I am crazy. They said the Bible drove me crazy. The Bible won't make you crazy."

Mildred had joined us. "Chaplain, this woman here can look you straight in the eye and tell if you've got good sense." Then, turning to the woman who had interrupted us, she asked, "Does the chaplain have good sense?"

The woman drew closer and gazed into my eyes, then answered, "Yes."

"Do I have good sense?" Mildred asked her.

Again the woman drew close, gazed into Mildred's eyes, and answered, "Yes."

Still another patient motioned to me with her hand. "Come sit here; I want to tell you something." She had a lovely face, blonde hair, and a soft voice. She was probably in her fifties. "I'm not crazy," she began. "I've got as much sense as you have. I want you to help me."

"How can I help you?"

"They are sending those electronics and flying saucers over here from the main building. One hit me on top of my head, and I want you to stop them 'cause they hurt me."

"I'll be glad to help whenever I can."

She smiled pleasantly and thanked me.

I walked on but stopped by the side of another woman in tears. She tried to speak but couldn't. I waited. Soon she wiped her eyes with the hem of her skirt. "Chaplain, I'm not mentally sick. I'm brokenhearted. I'm only 36; I'm not crazy. I can remember everything. I'm brokenhearted by the way I've been taken away from my children. I can see my baby being mistreated. I've just been pushed in the mud. They locked me up in jail." She began crying softly again. "Everything I've lived for is gone, gone, gone," she sobbed.

I waited, my heart filled with compassion for her.

"This is the question," she continued, "what have I done to be put in a place like this? I've tried to make peace. I still have my husband and would go back to him if he would treat me right. I'm never going to get out of here. I know it. My husband said he was going to let me stay here and rot." The poor despondent woman began sobbing again. When she finally dried her tears, I tried to comfort her.

"It may not be as bad as it seems. Your husband probably was angry when he said that, and wanted to hurt you. He may cool off and see it differently. Time heals all hurts. And there are other ways to get out of the hospital if your husband refuses to take you out. The doctor and social worker can help you on this at the proper time."

She wiped her reddened eyes once more with the hem of her skirt, then, holding my hand in hers, smiled and said, "Thank you. You have helped me."

Joyce Savage introduced herself to me and said, "Chaplain, did you ever see so many nutty people?" I smiled but didn't answer. "You ought to be thankful you're not mentally ill," she added.

"I am thankful, Mrs. Savage."

"This mental illness is something awful," she explained. "You can't really know unless you've had it."

THROUGH THESE EYES

"No, I'm sure you're right."

"Do you think it's God's will that anyone be crazy or mentally ill, whatever we call it?"

"No, indeed. It is not in God's plan for anyone. He wants us to be mentally *well*."

She asked further, "Do you think God will hold us responsible for what we do after we've lost our minds?"

"Why do you ask?"

"Well, I have trouble remembering things. My mind isn't clear like it was."

"No, Mrs. Savage, you haven't lost your mind. You've still got lots of sense. We all forget things. You may happen to be confused a bit in your thinking, but I feel that will clear up and you will be all right again."

"Thank you. I feel lots better since you told me that," she smiled at me.

I waved my hand to her as I left, saying, "I will see you again soon."

Down the hall I came to a patient who was busy wiping the walls with a wet cloth. "My, but you are busy!" I commented. "There are no lazy bones in you."

"It helps me to feel needed," she said. "If I didn't have some work to do, I'd be as crazy as a betsy bug." She laughed and said, "I may be crazy, but I don't think I'm completely off my rocker."

I exited the ward, thinking, Most of the mentally ill, like all the rest of us, believe they are sane.

-14-

D. W. had been a patient for a long time. During his years at the hospital he had held many of the jobs done by those patients who worked: cleaning bathrooms, serving in the dining room, farm labor.* He was always present for church services.

"Chaplain," he said to me, "I've been here 17 years. I've had one visit during that time; my sister came at Christmas once to see me. I've cried and worked and prayed. I enjoy going to church here. Everyone is good to me. The food is good. But I would like a trial visit home."

Another man remarked, "Chaplain, something strange is going on around here. I asked the doctor about going home. He said I could go home if my people would write him first about me going home. Then when my people came to see me, they said they would come for me when the doctor says I'm ready to go home. Looks to me like they're giving me the run-around."

Another fellow spoke up. "I hear they're going to open the doors and let us all out of here."

---

* See footnote on patients' work on page 73.

"Why?" I asked.

"'Cause we're getting overcharged with electricity," he replied.

A younger patient standing nearby lifted his right forefinger to his head, made a circular motion with it, and said, "You're crazy. You know that they're not going to do any such thing." He paused, then added, "Chaplain, when are they going to let me go home? I'm getting so much sense, I don't know what to do with it. I learn so much sitting around and listening." I agreed with him that there is much we learn by being here.

"I want to go home, too, like the rest of these fellows," said an intelligent-looking patient. "Just about everyone here has the going-home fever. Wouldn't it be wonderful if we could all go home?" Then, looking directly at me, he added, "It would leave all of you without a job. You wouldn't mind it though, would you, chaplain?"

"Absolutely not," I answered.

"I've had some wonderful experiences here—and some bad ones," he reflected. "But life is like that anywhere we are, isn't it?"

"True."

"When I first came here I thought I knew everything and that the doctor was stupid. Now I realize I was the stupid one. I've made a lot of progress in my understanding since coming here."

I agreed with him. "There's always room for improvement for all of us and we can do it when we are willing to try."

"We sure can," he replied, and several men sitting and standing nearby nodded their heads and added their assent to his.

"Fellows, I must go," I said, realizing the time. "I've enjoyed being with you."

"Come back to see us, chaplain, every time you can. You have no idea how much your visits mean to us," said the man with the intelligent countenance.

I went to an area which was used by patients to receive visits from their families.

"Chaplain, I want you to meet my husband," a woman called. Her husband, a middle-aged man, balding, overweight, and with shifty eyes that would not meet mine, exchanged greetings with me, then walked away from us.

"Chaplain," his wife began, "I've just got to get back home to my child."

"But the doctor says you aren't well enough to go home yet."

"I don't care what the doctor says. I've got to go to my child," she said with strong feeling.

"That means going back home to your husband, too," I reminded her, recalling that she had told me she would never live with her husband again. "Are you ready to go back to him?"

"No, I'm not," she said emphatically. "I don't want to go back to one who is always holding a hammer over my head and a sword at my throat."

As I left her, I heard a ward attendant call out to another patient, "Betty, you have a visitor; your mother is here."

"Oh, I hope she gets to go home," exclaimed someone else. Then she added, "I want to go home. I've got five children; they need me." Tears came to her eyes.

Betty's mother had come by bus from a distant part of the state to see her daughter. They kissed and the mother showed Betty a new dress and underwear she had brought for her. The two women held the clothes up to see if they would fit, then they sat down and ate a sack lunch together. Betty told her mother, "I want to go home, but if you don't want me there I can go to Norfolk and live with Aunt Mamie."

"Who gave you the idea I don't want you home?" her astonished parent asked.

"That's what some of the patients say. They said if you wanted me home you'd come and get me."

"You shouldn't pay any attention to what they say, Betty.

I've talked with your doctor and he says you aren't well enough yet. When he says so, I'll be right here for you."

"I get so tired sitting here on the ward, day after day, with nothing to do," Betty sighed.

On another occasion, as I entered one of the women's wards, I heard a young patient saying loudly, "I didn't think I loved my husband but I could love a rattlesnake if that would get me out of here." Seeing me, she said, "Chaplain Thomas, I want to see my baby. I've been here a month. If I could just hold my baby for a few minutes. . . ." She began crying softly. "I want to see my baby. I want you to talk to my doctor about me going home. You must have lots of influence over him. Get him to let me go home to my husband and my baby."

She reached into a pocket and withdrew a photograph. "Here's my baby's picture. I don't need to be here. I need to be home taking care of my baby." I admired the handsome child in the photograph, then she turned and showed it to several ladies.

A brunette grasped my hand and said, "I want to go *home*." She drew the word home out in a tone of desperate longing.

A patient who had recently returned from a visit home said, "All we talk about is going home. Then we come back. When I go again, I'm never coming back to this place. I'm going to burn my bridges behind me when I leave. I think I've learned to behave myself." She was a pretty woman in her thirties.

The brunette spoke again, "Can't you help me get to my children and my husband? My husband has ulcers and there's no one there to cook for him. He needs me more than I need to be here. Isn't there something you can do to help me?" she pleaded.

"What do you want me to do?"

"Can't you talk to the doctor for me? I can't catch him to talk to him; he goes through here like a breeze."

"The doctor will write to your husband to come for you when he thinks you are ready to go," I tried to reassure her.

"I'm as well as I can be," she insisted. "If I stay here much longer, I'll crack up for sure. I'm not kidding either. I can't stand all these folks and all this cursing and noise. I'm not used to such." She paused a moment and added, "Well, at least I know my husband loves me and wants me home as soon as the doctor will release me."

One of the ladies commented, "We have it good here. Everyone is nice to us and we are fed well, but we'd rather be home."

"There's certainly no place like home," I wholeheartedly agreed.

"I guess I'm stuck here for life," said a small woman in her late thirties. "I've been a jailbird and a mental patient. If I ever get out of here, maybe I can get a job mixing drinks."

Another patient spoke up, "I don't know why Dr. Rivers keeps me here. I feel better than I've felt in ten years. There's nothing wrong with me except I'm homesick. I'm so homesick I can taste it."

"How does it taste?" I gently teased her.

"Well, it sure doesn't taste good!" she replied.

I walked on down the ward and was stopped by Ruth, who said, "I've got to get out of this honky-tonk place. This is no place for me. I'm a nice woman of good character; I don't belong on this ward with all these whores." There was a note of desperation in her voice. She had been at the hospital for 11 years and I had heard this from her many times. I always tried to listen.

Helen spoke up and said, "My daddy is dead. My mother lives alone. I wrote her to let me come home and that I would be good. I told her I live here on this ward with over 100 women and I never hurt anyone. I told her if I could live here with all these, I ought to be able to live with her. She wrote me she'd think about it. She says she's afraid of me 'cause I hurt her once."

Mattie pleaded her case. "I came here to get well, but I'm anything else now. These treatments have made me a lot worse.

They don't solve any of my problems. I've no place to go. I've done so sorry, I feel no one wants me. Ever since I've been here I've been through hell. They told me if I'd be good, I'd soon go home. I've been good, but they won't take me home. I've been here four years. I'd rather be dead than stay on here. I'm to blame. I must have been crazy to let those things happen. I dated my husband's cousin. I shouldn't have done it." (Mattie had had many shock treatments and tranquilizing drugs. One night, some time later she died alone in her room; she had hanged herself with a bed sheet.)

An elderly woman, a bit feeble, held my hand and said, "I don't belong here. There's nothing wrong with my mind. I want you to write my folks to come after me."

"That's the doctor's responsibility. Have you talked to him about it?"

"I never get a chance to talk to him. He goes through here so fast. I tried to stop him once by tripping him," she smiled, "but he jumped over my foot."

"I want to go home, too," said a former schoolteacher. "I don't see why I should be here just because I'm old. My people aren't the kind to put anyone here and forget them, but I've been here three years. Can you help me?"

I was always ready to help whenever I could, but never did I feel so helpless as at times like this. I knew, however, that I could give patients a warm smile and handshake and try to listen understandingly. I knew that these people needed someone to whom they could express their true feelings.

The former teacher continued, "I want to get out of here. It's so pitiful here. You hardly find more than one or two old people in a home, but here there are hundreds. It's killing me." She handed me a writing tablet to look at. "I've been writing down some scriptures: 'I am the way, the truth and the life. . . . Ye shall know the truth and the truth shall make you free. . . . God is spirit and those who worship him must worship him in spirit and in truth.'"

I read the words and she said, "If I can write that, you know my mind is all right." Then she recited from memory the squares of all the whole numbers from one to 25. "You know that my mind is all right if I can do that. This is just no place for me. I'd like to be out and doing something useful. I don't have a hole in my head. This should prove it. You see I deserve to be out of a place like this."

"Does anyone ever go home from here?" someone asked.

"Oh, yes, some go home everyday," I assured her.

Clapping her hands together, Sally came up to me and said, "The doctor says I can go home! I'm glad; I need to be with my children and they need me."

"We are glad for you, Sally," I answered with joy.

"He has just told me I can go as soon as my husband comes for me. I guess he's decided I've got enough sense to go home."

Sarah said sadly with a sob in her voice, "I wish I could go home but I can't. My folks don't want me. I've been banished from society."

Mrs. Elm, a jolly, buxom lady came over and took my hand. Kissing the back of it, she said, "I'm going to do something for you that Satan has never done. I'm going to leave you."

"How do you know that Satan has never left me?"

"I can tell by your conversation." She laughed and I joined in with her. "I'm going home next week," she continued. "It's been good knowing you. You certainly have helped make my two years here a lot brighter. We'd all get mighty lonely without you, Chaplain Thomas."

A Mrs. Williamson spoke up. "Chaplain, I've been here over 28 years. That seems like enough for me. I want to go home." I agreed with her that 28 years was indeed a long time, and she continued, "I've prayed every prayer that's in the Bible but I'm still here. Write my people to come for me; tell them I want to go home." I wondered if she still had living relatives, if they wanted her at home, and even if she would not feel very dissatisfied at home after living here so long.

Bryce patients who died without family or friends are buried in the hospital cemetery.

"Mrs. Williamson, some day you *will* go home—if not to your earthly home, then to your heavenly home. Then there will be no more of this."

"I'm so proud you stopped to talk with me. You have no idea how proud I am to see you each time you come through here." Mrs. Williamson had been clinging to my hand, and she slowly released her hold as she looked into my face.

I keenly sensed how deep was the loneliness many patients felt in their separation from home and all it meant. Some wept out of homesickness and openly expressed it, but many others' hearts were gripped with a great and silent fear that they were here in the hospital for the remainder of their days.

-15-

" D o you think I'll go to hell?"

That was the question put to me as I entered the disturbed ward. The questioner was a middle-aged woman, thin, slightly stooped, and wearing a disapproving expression. She looked hard at me, at my suit, at my hair combed smoothly back. I smiled, and with difficulty she smiled back faintly.

"Let's sit here and talk about your question, Mrs. Grayson," I said, motioning her to a bench. "Why do you think you will go to hell?"

"I've committed the unpardonable sin."

"What do you think is the unpardonable sin, Mrs. Grayson?"

"I've been unfaithful to my husband and lived with this other man. Isn't that the unpardonable sin?" she asked.

"No, Mrs. Grayson, that is not the unpardonable sin."

"Then what is it?" she asked further.

"I'm not sure I know. There's been a lot of confused thinking on the subject. But of this I am sure: as long as you feel bad about having done what you did and wish you had not done it, you have not committed the unpardonable sin."

"I'm so miserable. I know I've done wrong. I've committed

adultery and I'm going to hell," she persisted.

"Mrs. Grayson, the church and society condemn the act of adultery, and rightfully so. But God loves you and forgives you." I talked on about God's love and forgiveness, but she was too confused to understand. My heart filled with compassion for Mrs. Grayson and I tried to console her, assuring her that she would be all right. She only answered by moaning and crying, "But you don't understand. You can't understand. Look at me. Here I am in the crazy house." Her remorse was so great that no word of comfort could penetrate her mind.

Many of those who have lost their way and come to the mental hospital seem to do so because of a wrong emphasis in religious teaching: religious leaders and others have filled their minds with fear. Good souls have become confused, bewildered, perplexed—even extremely terrified. Much of my time and effort as chaplain was given to trying to reconstruct the faith of those who came to the hospital. I continually tried to help patients realize that God loves each of us—not because we are good, nor because we are bad—but because it is his nature to love.

I left Mrs. Grayson and went to speak to a new patient sitting quietly in a rocking chair. She told me her name was Eliza Jane Morris. The information card which I had about her stated that she was single, aged 54, and her occupation was housework. I asked, "Would you tell me why you came here?"

"I've had so much on me," she answered in a small voice.

"Would you like to tell me more about it?"

"I'm the father of all the churches in the world," said she. "The Lord has put on me a heavy responsibility, but I promised him I'd do my best."

"How did the Lord come to choose you, Miss Morris?"

"Because I'm so humble and lowly. He said he had searched the whole universe and that I'm the only little sister he found who was meek and lowly." She spoke in tones that were sweet and unassuming.

"You indeed have great responsibility upon you," I replied.

"Yes, the Lord's put me above him, above the whole world. As his little sister, I can go around the world in 50 minutes."

"That's some travelling, Miss Morris."

"Yes, it is, honey—if I should call you that. You see, you are my child."

"I'm very glad to have met you, Miss Morris. If I can help you in any way while you are here, feel free to call upon me."

I joined a woman whom I recognized as another newcomer to the hospital. I told her my name and she introduced herself as Mrs. Edna Barrett. She was tall, buxom, gray-haired, and immaculate in appearance. She wore no makeup. Her admission card gave her age as 56. When Mrs. Barrett came to the hospital she was crying and had to be forced by the attendants to go to her ward. Her appearance was unkempt.

"How are you getting along, Mrs. Barrett?"

"I've been awfully nervous. I used to be so happy. Now I'm not. I tried to commit suicide. I lost my husband about four years ago. I found him dead in the backyard. That was a terrible blow to me. I've done something I shouldn't have done: I had an affair with a married man this past year. I liked his attention and was very happy when I was with him. I began to have guilt feelings and felt I was doing something terribly wrong. Several other men wanted to come and see me, and did once or twice.

"I feel hostile toward my mother. She tried to interfere with my activities. All my neighbors were watching me and ridiculing me. It made me very nervous. I think it's better for me to get away from it all so I won't have to think about what I've done. I used to have faith in God and people, but I don't anymore."

"Mrs. Barrett, you may have lost faith in God, but he still has faith in you. He loves each of us still, no matter who we are, where we are, or what we have done. It is for each of us to turn to him and become aware of his eternal presence and everlasting love. There is no better use you can make of your time while here at the hospital than to do just that." Mrs. Barrett thanked

THROUGH THESE EYES

me for talking with her and I turned to speak with others.

Without any formalities, an elderly lady standing nearby said sadly, "They've poisoned me three times here. They've killed my three children. Looks like they're not going to let me out. This is an awful place. If I ever get out, you'll never see me down here again." She sat down in a chair. I asked her name and she said it was Ruby Nell Walker. "There's nothing wrong with my mind. I'm just old and my children chucked me away here."

"Thank you for telling me these things, Mrs. Walker," I replied. "Even when our children cast us aside the Lord will lift us up."

"That's all I have to hold on to."

"I'll be back to see you, Mrs. Walker. God loves you."

I turned to speak to Alice Mazer. She, too, was ready to tell me of her miserable condition. "I had a good husband and home, plenty of money, plenty of everything. My husband fell dead right in front of me. He was a widower with two children when I married him. Those children came in and took everything away from me. It all went in a night. Those old doctors said my nerves gave way. They tricked me and gave me dope. I've got better two times, then the doctors gave me more dope. I told a lady preacher last Sunday that I was headed here to see if I could get help. She told me that anyone who came here was devil-possessed. They haven't done anything here for me.

"I've been very unlucky with husbands. I married one. We lived together 21 years. He died suddenly. I married another. He was a dope addict, so I divorced him. Then I lived 12 years with this last husband. Some said I had been living in adultery with this man since my husband that I divorced was still living. I've felt guilty about that and worried a lot about it. I haven't lost my mind. I'm just nervous. I might have done better not to have come here."

After speaking a few reassuring words to Mrs. Mazer, I joined Mrs. Dorcas Matthews who was shuffling feebly past us. Her voice was weak and complaining. "My husband died a year ago. Since then I've felt depressed and lonely. I just cry myself to sleep. That doesn't do any good. I'd rather be dead than suffer the mental agony I endure. Nobody has treated me right. My daughter quarrels at me and won't let me have any of my money. She says I'd lose it. My children wanted me to come here. I don't know if I should have come or not. I've had so much trouble. I guess I'll be down here the rest of my life."

"Mrs. Matthews," I said, trying to give her comfort and assurance, "I'm not sure. You may have to be here the rest of your life, but believe me when I say that God loves you and will be with you to sustain you. Someday he will say, 'You've suffered enough, Mrs. Matthews. Come up higher.' Then you will be free from all the tears and heartaches and disappointments of this life."

I noticed Dorothy Palmer, a neat, younger woman, sitting in a rocking chair and talking to another patient who listened indifferently. Mrs. Palmer was very hostile when she came to the hospital and had to be led forcibly to a ward. Hostility showed today in the tone of her voice as she told her story, a story she had repeated many times to anyone who happened to be nearby.

"I'm being held here as a hostage. There's nothing wrong with my mind. I invented that thing that's going around the world. It's so terrific. I've been bribed, swindled, and everything else. I think it's time for me to get out of here, as important a person as I am. I'm not a person to be in a place like this. I've got so much to do. I don't know why I'm being held in this dungeon. I'm losing $1 million each day I'm held a prisoner. I'm due in Washington now. I'm the richest woman in the world. I now have over $700 billion. My invention is mental therapy, but the doctors won't use it." Her indifferent companion seemed unimpressed.

I met and talked with all the newly arrived patients on the ward and greeted others with a smile and handshake, engaging in brief conversation with some. As I was about to leave, an attendant touched me on the arm. "Chaplain, Eloise Jackson is in her room. She heard your voice and wants to talk with you."

I found Mrs. Jackson lying on her bed, her entire body trembling. She was in her early forties, a brunette, the wife of a doctor and mother of three children. "I asked to be locked in my room," she began. "I'm so nervous, I feel like I want to run away. I'm afraid I'll hurt myself. If anyone ever needed a padded cell, I feel that I do. I have to hold myself to keep from crushing myself against the wall."

"Well, Mrs. Jackson, we do not have any padded cells, or straight jackets either."

Tears rolled freely down her cheeks as she continued. "I've tried to be a good woman all my life. I must have done something bad and God is punishing me for it."

"All of us make mistakes, Mrs. Jackson. Either ignorantly or knowingly, we have done things which may in later years bring suffering. God has so created us that we can bring good or evil into our lives, but God is good. He no more brings suffering upon us than we as loving parents would bring suffering upon our children."

I left her room and was accosted by a patient waiting for me in the hallway. "Chaplain, I sure need to talk to you," she said. Her name was Christine Ford, and she was a heavyset woman in her mid-thirties, neatly dressed, pleasant and cooperative. I had learned that when she came to the hospital she was incredibly dirty, barefooted, and extremely hostile toward her husband, whom she had married when she was 14 years old. She had a delusion that the welfare department was trying to take her children from her. Yet she would often walk away from home and leave her children alone, crying, while she hid in the woods. She resented her children and had threatened to kill both them and herself. She had to be watched so that she would not burn her house down.

Mrs. Ford spoke calmly to me, seeming eager to talk. "There's nothing wrong with my mind. I got angry with my husband, quit him and went to town. I got a job in a restaurant and a room to live in. The sheriff picked me up three days later and put me in jail for a week; then he brought me here." She laughed loudly and her brown eyes glistened as she recalled those events. "I sure beat them up in jail and fought like a tiger if anyone came near me. It took five of them to handcuff me to bring me here. I didn't want to come here."

She paused as if reflecting on the whole situation. I waited for her to continue. "My real husband died about seven years ago. He was an ex-soldier. I'm not married to this guy. We've been living together, off and on, for six years and he's living off the money my husband left me. This guy doesn't believe there's a God Almighty. One day he came in and saw me lying on the bed. We argued and he hit me on the head. I pushed him down. He got a lightbulb out of the socket and hit me on my arm. It broke. I picked up a piece of it and said, 'If you want me to bleed, I'll bleed.'" She pointed to five lacerations where she had cut her left wrist.

"When I get out of here, I'm going to be married to that guy or not go back to him. It's been on my conscience a long time. I've cried myself to sleep many nights about living in adultery. He doesn't want us to marry because if we do the $150 I get every month from my husband's pension will stop." Mrs. Ford had nothing more to add to her story. She thanked me for listening to her and I hurried to a conference room where I had an appointment with Loretta Evans.

I found her waiting for me. "Well, Mrs. Evans, what seems to be the trouble?"

"It's like this. I feel I was put here to stay. A doctor whom I've never known signed the paper for me to be brought here. There's no reason for me to be here. My husband—I don't call him my husband—he put me here. It's money and spite that put me here. I lived with him, not as a wife." Mrs. Evans was a neatly dressed woman of medium size with graying hair. She held a candy sucker on a stick in her hand, occasionally putting it to her mouth as she talked.

"Please do something for me, chaplain. Write my husband that I need to be at home so I can take care of things. And my pooch, my little dog. I want to see him. I don't love my husband after the way he beat me up. I'm an honest woman. He used to run around with other women. I don't know what he's doing while I'm here. He loves me in a warped sort of way. That kind of person will turn and destroy what he loves. I haven't heard from my son since I came here. He's 29."

Mrs. Evans paused and licked the sucker. "There were years that I couldn't smile. I longed for love and consideration. Before I came here, I finally got where I could smile again. I had a song in my heart and wings on my heels. Then I ended up here." Tears flowed down her cheeks. Wiping them with her hand, she said, "I mustn't get emotional; it's not good for me.

"I'd rather have schizophrenia or anything than this drug which I'm taking. I'm so depressed. I feel so sorry for myself. I find it hard to take care of my toilet or comb my hair. I don't love anyone now. I can't, like this." She lifted the sucker to her mouth again for a moment, then continued. "I don't have any confidence in that doctor. I asked him why he gave me that drug. He said I was nervous when I came here. He doesn't know that it's my nature to be gay. Will this drug make an idiot out of me?"

"No, Mrs. Evans, it will not make an idiot of you."

"It's about made an idiot of Barbara Gates. She's that girl on the ward with the blue dress on. You know her; she likes you. She was jolly, and now her mind is almost blank." Mrs. Evans placed her hand on her chest as she talked on. "That drug isn't doing me any good. I feel lots worse than I did when I came here. I feel all dead inside. I feel like I want to commit suicide, but I don't have the guts to do it." She licked the sucker again.

"These beds! I wouldn't put my dog in such a place. And

the pillow is a hard lump. My pooch has a very good bed. It's not lumpy like these beds. Being here just isn't for me. It's a waste of time. I'm just marking time by being here. Furthermore, I'm just using up the taxpayers' money."

I felt that our conference had lasted long enough, perhaps too long. I had listened attentively while she expressed her feelings about her husband, her pooch, the doctor, and the drug. Since she had not sought any specific help from me I offered none. Early in the interview she had suggested that I write her people, but did not pursue the thought. I had already written them my customary letter when she was admitted to the hospital. I rose to leave, stating that if I could help her further she should feel free to call upon me. She thanked me for coming and apologized for taking up so much of my time.

I had a brief visit to the wards on the third floor, preparing to leave the hospital for the day. As I stood exchanging greetings for a few minutes with three women, Mrs. Steele, an attendant, ran up and grabbed my arm. In a frightened voice she said, "Come here, quick! Look out the window at that man with a pistol in his hand. He just shot a man several times. He shot the man even after he had fallen down!"

Mrs. Steele and I rushed downstairs and cautiously went out on the front porch. As we passed the receptionist's desk, hospital personnel were using all available telephones, calling for a doctor, the director of nursing, the hospital superintendent, the police, and an ambulance.

Within a few minutes all were on the scene, where the apparently dead man lay stretched out on his back on the ground. Dr. Rivers placed his stethoscope over the man's heart. He was dead. Examination of his body showed a bullet wound in his hand, one in his neck, and several in his chest.

The attacker stood quietly by, holding an empty pistol pointed toward the ground. When asked his name by a policeman, he answered calmly, "Raymond. Harold B. Raymond." He was tall and lanky, probably in his early forties.

THROUGH THESE EYES

"How about letting me have the pistol?" asked the policeman. Raymond handed it over without a word.

"Who is this man you shot?" asked the law officer.

"Jack Landis."

"Why did you shoot him, Mr. Raymond?"

"I had to do it. My wife and my buddy and I brought my sister here to enter the hospital. A doctor had said she should be brought here for treatment. She's the wife of the man I shot. He hasn't lived with her for several months; they've been separated. He ran her crazy by his behavior. He heard we were planning to bring his wife—my sister—here. He said he'd shoot our guts out if we did.

"We've had trouble with him before. The law back where we live told us to come ahead. They said they didn't think he'd bother us, but to be safe we should come well armed just in case he tried any trouble. After we got my sister committed, he came up in his car. He jumped out when he saw us, caught my buddy by the arm and started pulling him over to his car, trying to keep my buddy between us. This thing has been building up inside me all day. I started shooting and I couldn't stop."

The dead man's car was searched and a loaded double-barreled shotgun found inside. Both it and the pistol were taken by the police as evidence. The ambulance carried the body of the dead man to a funeral home and the police carried the murderer to the local jail. The crowd soon dispersed.

During the proceedings I had glanced up at the hospital windows several times and seen many patients gazing out. Knowing that many of them were agitated under ordinary conditions, I went back to visit all the wards again and answer their questions. I hoped that my presence and a brief explanation would have a tranquilizing effect.

As I entered the first ward Mrs. Taggart, a small, elderly patient who was quite disturbed, came up close to me, pointed her finger at me, and shouted, "You've got policemen stationed around here shooting up the patients! We don't know who will be next. I want out of here and to go home. I've had all I can take." Her state of mind was such that any explanation of mine would be in vain, but Mrs. Galvin, a calmer lady, asked, "Just what happened?"

"It was a family fuss." I tried to speak distinctly enough so that all could hear. "Part of the family thought a woman should be brought here for treatment and another thought she should not. They shot it out and a man was killed."

"Is she here?" asked a patient.

"Yes, she is here, down on another ward."

"We're glad you came, chaplain," said someone. "We've never needed you like we do now."

The evening meal was called and I walked along with some of the ladies in the direction of the dining room. I asked Phyllis Nailer, who had been at the hospital several weeks, how things were going with her.

"Just fine, chaplain. It's not at all like what I expected. I used to have the idea that everyone here was really crazy: fighting, pulling hair, or butting their heads against the wall. I haven't seen anything like that in the three weeks I've been here, not even downstairs on the disturbed ward when I was there. After all I've been through, this is heaven to me."

Several ladies invited me to stay and eat with them, but I excused myself, saying that I must go home. As I passed by Dr. Rivers' office I looked in and found him cleaning blood off his stethoscope. "Well, chaplain, did you see the shooting?" he asked.

"No, but I saw Raymond holding the pistol and looking down at the dead man after he had emptied his gun into him."

"You know," Dr. Rivers mused, "if Raymond had not killed Landis, Landis might have killed one of us."

-16-

"Look! There goes a naked woman!" exclaimed a lady to her husband as they drove through the city's business district.

"Ah, you know it's no such thing," he replied.

"You can see for yourself. There she is going down the street. She has nothing but her stockings on and she's carrying a purse."

The naked woman came from a hotel. She had come down to the lobby a short time before to pay her bill. The desk clerk, a woman, had insisted that she come behind the counter until some clothes could be found. The guest had refused and sauntered away, passing through the coffee shop. She stopped at the side of a man who was sitting at a table typing. He looked up, saw her, then hastily dropped his head and continued typing furiously. The woman wandered out onto the sidewalk and into the drugstore next door. There the female clerk tried to get something on her and finally succeeded in wrapping a plastic raincoat about her. But the woman threw it aside and walked out into the chilly weather.

A secretary in a nearby office building said to her boss, "There goes a naked woman down the street."

"Listen, they've got a place at the mental hospital for folks who see things like that," he answered. He walked over to the window and looked out. "Well, it sure is. I guess they'd better make room for both of us over there."

A prominent lawyer caught up with the woman as she walked along, purse swinging and stockings flapping around her ankles. Offering her his raincoat, the attorney tried to wrap it around her shoulders. The woman threw it to the ground and stomped on it. Turning on him, she scratched his face, then grabbed his tie and was choking him when the police, who had been called by the hotel clerk, arrived on the scene. She turned her anger on them when they tried to arrest her. With great effort the policemen subdued her and took her to jail.

When I came home from the hospital that evening my wife, Clytie Mae, was reading the evening paper. After we greeted each other she asked, "Did you hear anything today about a nude woman being arrested on the street here and being committed to the hospital?"

"No, I did not."

"Here's an article about it," she said, handing over the local newspaper. It carried a brief statement: "Police Take Woman Into Custody Here. An unidentified white woman was taken into custody at noon today when she walked out onto the street in front of a downtown hotel dressed only in her stockings and carrying a purse in her hand. Police said she apparently was ill and would be taken to Bryce Hospital for detention and treatment until her people could be located."

When I had finished reading the article Clytie Mae continued, "This afternoon I was downtown on business. Nearly everywhere I went people asked me if I had heard about the incident and were laughing about it. I would reply, 'You know no woman in her right mind would dare do a thing like that, so of course she must be sick.' I told them that it could happen to any of us. It could have been our mother or daughter if mental illness were to overtake her."

"What did they say to that?"

"They said they had never thought of it that way before and maybe they were wrong in making fun of her."

I learned the next day that the police had taken the woman to the station house where they eventually were able to get some clothing on her. From there they carried her to Bryce. On arrival at the hospital she was dirty and dishevelled, crying and still fighting. Her left wrist had a small cut which had been self-inflicted. The woman was about 30 years old, five feet six inches tall, had brown hair, blue eyes and a clear complexion. She was robust and overweight. There were bruises on her body and injuries from her struggle with those who were trying to help her. She was extremely disturbed.

The commitment papers, signed by a doctor, read: "This woman will not tell her name. She came into the city yesterday. Today she nicked her wrist, inflicting a minor wound. She appeared in a hotel lobby undressed. The desk clerk called the police. The woman ran but was overtaken and forcibly taken to the city jail. There she beat on the walls, refused to put on clothes or give information to the police, and tore the policemen's clothing whenever they came within her reach. From the city jail she was taken to Bryce Hospital."

When Dr. Rivers went to the woman's room at Bryce to give her a physical examination he found her wandering about without any clothing and talking loudly. She threatened to hit him. She said she was going to kick and bite him. She was very profane and showed a great deal of hostility. She had to be restrained in order for him to examine her.

The examination showed no evidence of physical illness or of involvement with drugs or alcohol. Following the physical examination the woman was given sodium surital intravenously in an effort to obtain information about her. The attempt was unsatisfactory and she was given an electric shock treatment, then another one later in the day.

Two or three days later, Dr. Rivers reported at a staff meeting that the woman was showing considerable improvement.

Whereas she had been extremely disturbed, hostile, and belligerent, and would not wear her clothes, she had come out of her disturbed state and was pleasant and cooperative and fitting in well with the general routine.

Another article appeared on the front page of the newspaper three days after the first one. It said:

Ailing Woman's Identity Learned

A young woman who went out unclothed on our streets several days ago has been identified. Superintendent Sidney Tarwater of Bryce Hospital said that she is a resident of another state, and that she is to be transferred there soon for further treatment.

"When she was brought to us she was an extremely sick person," Dr. Tarwater said today. "We've done what we could to help her, and within the last few hours she has been able to provide information that led to her identity's being established."

He added that the young woman had no connection with our city and that she came here while travelling aimlessly after leaving her home. Arrangements were being made at the time of her disappearance to provide institutional care for her in her own state.

"The patient is the mother of two children. Her husband is greatly relieved to know her whereabouts and is planning to do everything he can to help his wife," Dr. Tarwater said.

A few days later I was passing through a hospital kitchen and stopped to speak with a patient who was putting cake on trays for the noon meal.

"I'm Melba Dixon," she said.

"And I'm Chaplain Thomas," I replied. I knew she was the woman mentioned in the newspaper articles, although we had never actually met before. Hospital personnel had been cautioned not to reveal the patient's identity to the public, but because of my position as chaplain I knew who she was.

Melba Dixon offered me a piece of cake and asked, "Did I mistreat you or say anything out of way to you when I first came here?"

"No, Mrs. Dixon. Why?"

"I hear I gave the doctors a pretty rough time. Dr. Rivers told me today that my husband is supposed to come for me this weekend. I'd like to begin all over. Reckon it's possible?"

"Perhaps it will be," I replied.

"Do you suppose my husband will take me back?"

"Why do you think he would not?"

"We haven't been living together as man and wife for several years," Mrs. Dixon explained.

"Why not?" I asked, refusing a second piece of cake.

"I was in love with another man, but we didn't go too far with it. If my husband will take me back, I'd be glad to try again."

"How do you account for this good feeling you now have, Mrs. Dixon, and for your willingness to start over?" I inquired.

"The shock treatments, I guess. Have you ever had one?"

"No."

Smiling, she said, "They knock something out of you."

I remembered that other work awaited me, so I thanked Mrs. Dixon for the cake and a very pleasant visit. On my way from the room I stopped by the desk and remarked to the attendant in charge that Mrs. Dixon was certainly getting along very well.

"Yes," she said, "she was bad sick when she came. She fought us like a tiger." Then, with emotion she added, "Our police department certainly has a bad leader. We're used to talking to these sick people who come here like they are humans. I hope I never have to deal with that man; we just wouldn't get along. He was trying to make her tell him her name. She didn't know it. Then he lit in on her, telling her she had hurt him when she fought him. He just doesn't understand how to deal with mentally ill people."

I started to leave, but she added, "By the way, there's a new lady here who has asked to talk with the chaplain."

"I can see her after lunch."

"Her name is Mrs. Bertice Lavender."

"I'm Chaplain Thomas. I believe you're Mrs. Bertice Lavender."

"Yes, I am," she said, extending her hand to me.

"I understand you asked to talk with me."

"Yes, I did. May we go into this room where we will not be interrupted, if you don't mind?"

Mrs. Lavender was a tall, slender woman. She had a rather dark complexion, coal black hair, brown eyes, and thick lips. Her movements and her speech were slow. She sat down on the lone bed in the room and I took the chair. She began talking easily.

"This is my sixth time in a mental hospital. I've been locked up in jail for six months. I was in reform school eight months. I've been married twice and am divorced now." Her voice rose higher and she spoke emphatically. "If I throw my body away and my soul in hell, that's *my* business. I'm 21 years old!" She paused, then continued more quietly, "I don't have any confidence in Dr. Rivers. He just believes in shock treatments, and I don't. I'm as afraid of shock treatments as I am of the devil himself."

Bertice shifted her body slightly.

"My father left home when I was six weeks old. He didn't reappear until I was 18. Long before that my mother had married a drunkard. As I grew older, my stepfather would make passes at me. When I came here I wasn't acting up. When I came here the first time it was my wedding day. At the front desk I pitched a hissy and ran away. It took four people to catch me and put me in here."

Bertice crossed her legs and continued, "A year ago I was a prostitute, a whore. I had just miscarried a baby and wanted a baby so much I was trying to get pregnant. Now I am pregnant—that's another story. I shouldn't have given myself to the dogs in the first place. My mother had me arrested, saying I was a vagrant. She should be arrested and put here 'cause she thinks everyone else is crazy. I have a mind of my own. I have a will of my own.

"I was on my way to being a prostitute. I thought I wanted to be one. I wanted to be a real good one like some of the other girls were so I could be choosy about my customers and make more money. On occasions I've had sex with as many as 25 or 30 men in one night and would make as much as $200. The charges were $5 for 15 minutes, $10 for 30 minutes, $15 for 45 minutes, and $20 for what they call a blow job. The prostitute's cut was three dollars out of every five. The madam told me I wasn't the kind for a whore. That really pleased me," she said, smiling.

"I hate men," Bertice added without raising her voice, "because my daddy went off and left me. Then my stepdaddy made passes at me. The boy I was going with when I was 14—he went off and married another girl, then sent me a wedding picture. My uncle was a drunkard and used vulgar language. I once did go in for that. He beat his children unmerciful, yet they grew up to be decent boys and girls.

"Then there are my two husbands. When I was married to the first one, I was in the hospital and needed blood. His matched mine. He wouldn't give it. He just left me in the hospital to live or die.

"My second husband took our three-year-old daughter out of my life. She's the only thing I ever really loved. I don't hate him for it, but I don't love him for doing it. Victoria, that's her name. She would tell her daddy, 'Mother is in the hospital. She will get well so she can take care of me.' She sent me some perfume back a month ago. It read, 'To the greatest mother in the world.' I know I'm not the greatest mother in the world, but my daughter is the sweetest thing in the world to me."

Pausing for a few minutes, Bertice continued as I listened closely to every word. "I was baptized as a girl. I believed in God. I've always believed in him. I've never done what he wanted me to do. That's where the sad story comes in. I'm not saying that because I'm talking with you. I don't have faith in God. I don't know why. I guess when you don't have confidence in yourself, you don't have confidence in anyone else. I don't like vulgar language, though I've used too much of it. Each night as I go to sleep, I pray, 'Oh, God, don't let anyone take this baby away from me. Let me keep it.'"

Straightening her back and looking directly into my eyes, Bertice said, "Chaplain Thomas, I'm not crazy. I'm just a mixed-up girl. If I am mentally ill, it's just meanness, mischief, and curiosity. I just need to repent. I know if I live the honky-tonk life, I'll burn in hell. But why should my mother and others get excited about it? It's my life to live. It will be me to burn in hell, not her. My mother thinks I don't care for my body—that's why I go out with men. I wouldn't do it if it wasn't for her trying to keep me from it.

"I'm no whore or prostitute. I used to be. God didn't give me my looks to use on men. He didn't give me my body for men to use. He gave me the things I have to use for good. I get scared to death every time I go to bed with a man. I think it's because of my stepfather. He never went all the way with me. He would hug me to himself and kiss me when Mother wasn't around or no one was looking. If he had never done that, I'd never have run away from home and be put in the reform school and then here."

She continued emphatically, "Dr. Rivers is stupid if he thinks electric shock treatments will cure what ails me. I've taken shock treatments and drugs. They've never helped me. I don't belong here. Two psychiatrists have told me there's nothing wrong with my mind.

"I know God loves me. I want a home that reflects love. Maybe that's expecting too much. Maybe I'll get it in heaven."

While I listened to Bertice and watched her, I saw kindness in her face. Feeling that she had talked enough, I said, "Yes, you are right, Bertice. You have not lived as God wants you to. But God loves you. He has not stopped loving you, nor will he ever stop. I believe there is something very fine in you. I believe you can be what God meant for you to be.

"God can help you to be that person, Bertice. You are still young, only 21. You remember the woman taken in adultery who was brought to Jesus? He told her, 'Neither do I condemn thee: go, and sin no more.'* He neither condoned nor approved her act. But if Jesus didn't condemn her, neither have I the right to condemn you. Jesus said he didn't come to condemn but to save. Do you remember the story? Jesus believed in the possibility of her rising above her past actions."

Bertice, seeming to ignore my words, asked, "Would you like to know why I believe as I do?"

"Yes, I would, if you care to tell me."

"I'm planning to write a book and put all my experiences in it. I'm 21, and when I'm 30, I'm going to settle down and write the book."

"Do you think the public will be interested in reading it?"

"There's lots of stuff of this kind on the newsstands and in books," she answered.

I tried to redirect her thoughts. "Bertice, the Bible tells us that of our own selves we can do nothing; it is God within us who does good works. We are to acknowledge him in all our

---

* John 8:11, King James Version

ways and he will direct our paths. Remember this, Bertice, your life is your own. It's up to *you* to choose what you do with it."

She smiled and extended her hand to me as I stood up to leave. "I thank you for coming to see me."

I closed the door behind me, leaving her to live with her old thoughts, ways, and desires, or to choose a better way of life.

-17-

A truck driver delivered several hundred live chickens which Bryce had purchased for food. Because he was unfamiliar with the grounds, he asked directions from a man standing in the yard.

"I need to talk to Dr. Tarwater. I have his chickens for him."

"I'm the man you're looking for."

"Where do I unload the chickens?"

"Right here's okay."

The driver scratched his head, shrugged, then did as he was told. As he opened the cages one after the other, with feathers flying, chickens flapped and squawked their way to freedom, randomly fluttering and disappearing into the bushes, under parked cars, and around the corners of buildings.

The driver took his invoice to the business office and there he met the real Dr. Tarwater. The man explained about the chickens, only to learn that he had been speaking with Tom Hubbard, a patient who had ground privileges—and *no* authority.

This is the story as it was told to me.

When I began my work at Bryce, Tom Hubbard was in his mid-fifties, a gray-haired man of average weight and build who carried himself erectly. Although friendly and good-natured, he preferred to spend most of his time alone, enjoying his own company and interests. He was a great reader, regularly salvaging professional journals which the cleanup crews had removed from the doctors and dentist's trash cans. He read the journals closely, and on one occasion quoted current information that was unfamiliar to a visiting dentist.

Tom had opinions on many subjects and expressed them readily, but he didn't require others to agree with him. His manner was courtly and gentlemanly and he had a lively sense of humor, which sometimes expressed itself in bawdy ways.

As he grew older, Tom put on weight around his midriff. He got a kick out of visiting the men in the hospital print shop where he had once worked; there he would draw himself to attention, salute snappily, and suck in his stomach—then laugh uproariously as his pants dropped to the floor.

One of Tom Hubbard's sisters came to my office one morning to talk to me about her brother and explain why she had had him committed. "I love my brother and I took care of him for years. No one else in the family would do it.

"To begin with, Tom Hubbard was a pack rat. He saves everything; in his bedroom there was only a path from the door to the bed. The rest of the room was waist deep in newspapers, boxes, string, decaying food and I-don't-know-what-else. After our mother died, he took over her room with his junk. Then he started putting stuff in my room. I put a stop to that right away."

"You really were patient with him."

"I've put up with a lot, but the last straw came when I hired a man to paint my house. The day he came I had to go to town for groceries and I left the painter with my brother. While I was gone Tom came out of the house and told the painter to come down from the ladder. The painter told Tom I'd hired him to paint the house. Then Tom threatened to pull the ladder out from under him if he didn't come down. After that I couldn't even leave the house anymore. I felt like he'd do something stupid or dangerous. I just couldn't take care of him any longer." "I understand. There's just so much one can take." "I felt I should talk to you about Tom. I love my brother and I want you to know that I haven't abandoned him." I told her that I knew her brother, that I had already met him.

Miss Hubbard continued, "I've brought him a box of little wrapped packages of cheese. He likes cheese, but I don't know if he eats it or saves it." She rose to leave. "I'm really glad I got to meet you. Please look after my brother." We shook hands and she left.

I found out through the years that Tom didn't eat all the cheeses. A ward attendant told me that occasionally he found little individually wrapped triangles of cheese squirrelled about the hospital.

In the late 1950's the hospital hired its first associate chaplain, Adolph L. Blakeney. It was decided that I would work with the female patients and Rev. Blakeney would work on the men's side.

One day he was called to the Psychology Department, where he was told that Tom Hubbard had asked to give a speech to the state legislature, and the department had had him make a recording of it. Rev. Blakeney listened to the tape and then sought Tom out. From that time until the mid 1970's, Tom would often rendezvous with the visitor tours led by Rev. Blakeney and give speeches—about mental illness, or the Alabama legislature, or patriotism.

After receiving his doctoral degree, Adolph Blakeney taught at The University of Alabama at Birmingham. He often took Tom Hubbard to Birmingham to address the students in his counselling and psychological testing classes there, and at other institutions also.

The following is a transcript of Tom Hubbard addressing one

of these class sessions during the 1970's—years of sweeping changes in the mental health field, and at Bryce in particular:*

Mental illness is relative. Mental illness is relative and circumstances alter cases.

When Henry Ford started to build his first automobile in his backyard in Michigan, his wife thought he was crazy and the neighbors thought he had gone nuts. Now suppose, instead of the turn of the century, suppose this had been much more recently. The chances are he might have spent the rest of his natural life in Bryce Hospital. The proverbial "tin Lizzy" might have died in the act of being born, and the people of America might never have known what they had missed.

Mental illness is relative and circumstances alter cases. Let a beautiful girl stand beside the highway and pull her skirts up above her waist and people would look at each other and shake their heads. Somebody would say, "Undoubtedly she is insane." But let those same people go down to the bathing beach and observe that same girl attired in nothing but an ultramodern bathing suit and their reaction would be quite different. Then you could probably see a great deal more in the case with the bathing suit than you could in the other. Mental illness is relative and circumstances alter cases.

Some years ago back home, a girl we had known since early childhood came over and spent the evening with my sister and me. We had recently lost our mother, and my sister and I were sorrowful and lonely. We had been recon-

---

* See footnote on commitment procedures on page 14.

ciled, but I had still been groping around for something tangible to hold on to. The thought came to me—and I think now it came as a revelation from on high—the thought that they who are anxious about death should remember and try to realize it is as much of an ordeal to be born as it is to die. To die is just a reverse process from being born—we've all been born. To die is just like being born, only in the reverse order.

This nice lady was visiting with us and I was in a talkative mood. I spoke of how the physical body I had when I was five years old had long since gone back to the dust of the earth, as surely as I had died, as though I had died and been buried in the grave when I was five years old. I'm the same person I was then and have the same personality, but the human physical body I had then is no more. It has gone the way of all the earth. I don't live in it anymore. There are those who would challenge this and say the body you now have is the same body you had, only grown larger. Well, the scientists claim that the human body completely renews itself every seven years. Every molecule and every atom is different. Even the bones are different. According to that, you and I have already died several times, but the process was so gradual as not to be noticeable. During every hour of every day and through the long night while we're asleep, this process continues, the process of throwing off the old and putting on the new. And every time we take a bath we wash off certain exuded particles that were the by-product of the process of throwing off the old and putting on the new.

My conversation was thuswise at some length. And later on that night when my sister and I were alone together she said, "Brother, I wish you would please never again embarrass me with your crazy talk." Well, I didn't answer. I just let the matter drop. But not many days after that, my sister and this lady who had spent the evening with us attended church together. My sister came home that day with her face all radiant with smiles and she said, "Brother, I'm so glad you said just what you did the other night. The preacher stood up there in the pulpit and said just about what you said the other night. He would say so the same way you did and all. And this girl sitting next to me was all in astonishment and wanted to know what on earth—had he been talking to your brother? I'm so glad you said just what you did the other night."

Well, in the first instance, I was her crazy brother with whom she had been sorely vexed and sorely embarrassed. In the other instance, I was now her illustrious brother of whom she was now immensely proud. All of which serves to illustrate once more: mental illness is relative and circumstances alter cases.

That's all of that speech. Now, do you want me to give the other speech now?

Upon receiving an affirmative response from his audience, Hubbard continued:

This other speech is a speech to the Alabama Legislature. You may or may not have heard of the guy who came from so far back in the woods they use 'possums for yard dogs, owls for chickens, boll weevils for plowhands. Well, think this one over. If someone had told you a few years ago that one of these United States of America had a vote fraud promoter for a circuit solicitor, a convicted murderer for one of its chief deputies, and an idiot for attorney general, you wouldn't have believed it, would you?

We know that following the line of least resistance makes men and rivers crooked. And the headwaters of Phenix City politics* are in Montgomery. I can understand how certain members of my family should want to get rid of me on a permanent basis. And I can understand how the management of Bryce Hospital and the doctors should be inclined to want to give me the kind of babysitter service they are required by law to give.

But there's one event that for the life of me I cannot understand: how a legislative body composed of intelligent men could deliberately enact a law** which violates our Bill of Rights and jeopardizes and threatens the constitutional right of every man, woman, and child in this state. And you could never convince me that they did this innocently, because they are not that ignorant. What kind of man could ever have introduced such a measure as this to the legislature, I cannot imagine. But this much I know for sure— it was a racketmonger and a scoundrel.

Long years have gone their weary way

---

* A reference to crime and corruption in this east Alabama border town during the 1930's and '40's.

** See footnote on commitment procedures on page 14.

since first I came to that valley of forgotten souls, and in the interim I have thought very much. Sometimes in the evening, while the lengthening shadows fall, I like to stand in the window and look at the mountains far away and watch the western sky. On some of these occasions my thoughts have drifted back to a time long ago when life was meaningful. And I have asked myself time and again who among us would want to face an unpurposeful future. Should a flower be born to bloom unseen and spend its fragrance on the desert air? What wouldn't I give this spring to walk along a sunlit path beside a meandering stream, there to cast in a hook and catch speckled trout or maybe a bass or two; or to stand on the edge of a great forest on a summer night, watching the stars shining overhead and listening to the song of the katydids.

[This is] the rightful heritage of every American—and yet where I am concerned, the self-appointed dictators of the Alabama gestapo have ruled it out. And then through the iron bars there appears a golden sunset, [with] its bright promise for a fair tomorrow, and hope springs eternal in the human breast.

You ask me what I think of Bryce Hospital. It's a straightforward question and deserves a straightforward answer. As a first-class free hotel I think it's ultrasuper. As a political football for a billion dollar racket, I think it's lousy. I thank you ladies and gentlemen.

The audience applauded and Hubbard continued:

Now we come to the dessert, the part of

THROUGH THESE EYES

the program I really do like—the question and
answer period. You're supposed to ask the questions and I'm supposed to give the answers.
Don't anybody be bashful; it's nobody here but
us. You may have ideas you've thought of and
wondered about, questions you'd like to ask.
Now's your chance. If there's discussion, they
say if you take an active part, you get more out
of something.

QUESTION: Do you like to read a lot?
ANSWER: Yes. I read quite a bit. When I was working at the
engineer's office I was very fond of the *Reader's Digest*, and if I
would sit in the window and try to read and I'd have an inter-
ruption every five minutes just about. But now, since I retired
from the engineer's office, I can sit out in the shade near my
ward and read many articles—well, a few anyway, without in-
terruption. And that seems much better that way. I like other
publications also, including the Bible and the encyclopedias. At
home I used to study the encyclopedia. When I was a child our
parents had the idea that a child in the home is worth two in the
street. And we had in our home a fine library, including the
Bible and several sets of the world's finest encyclopedias. And
evenings my sisters and I have spent in our library at home,
studying and reading. I was the only boy in a large family of
girls.

Maybe that takes care of that question.

QUESTION: Could you give us a brief history on how you came
about being a resident at Bryce?
ANSWER: Well, ah, I engaged in some activities that were, ah, at
variance with my sisters' ideas. I was the only boy in a large
family of girls and, almost as far back as I can remember, each
one of my sisters has considered herself a committee of one to
take care of little brother. And through the years they gave me

babysitter service, but they soon tired of that and wanted hire-
lings to do so. Finally they wanted Bryce Hospital to do so free
of charge.

Let's see now—ideas of how I came to Bryce Hospital. One
man asked me, "How did you get here?" I said, "Jaywalking,"
and he said, "anybody that jaywalks in that city belongs here."
Well, I have said that to people and they go off and tell that to
people—that they got in here for jaywalking. Then I have to
correct them, 'cause I was "goin' on" when I said that, something about like jaywalking.

One little trick I used to do—when I was much younger than
I am now and very fond of the ladies. I would pick up the phone
and dial just any number at random. If a man answered the
phone I'd say, "Please excuse—must have been a wrong number." If a nice young girl answered, I would go ahead and en-
gage her in conversation. I'd say, "Who is this?" Some of them
would slam up the phone in my face, but about nine out of ten
would tell me their first names. And I'd go ahead and talk to
them, and I'd have a mental note of the number I dialed and I'd
know her first name and her phone number. I'd say, "May I call
you sometimes?" And some of them would say, "I wouldn't
touch you with a ten-foot pole." But about nine out of ten would
say, "I'd like for you to." Well, I discovered that I had a voice
and that my voice had a way with women, and this became a
habit with me. And I'd call these girls and they'd respond over
the phone, and I had many girls at various times, and I'd say,
"When can I call you?" She'd say, "Anytime you want to," and
I'd call back from time to time. I had girls I talked to every
night.

I remember one night I felt in the mood for this. There was
a girl I liked and she liked me. She would call me one night and
I'd call her the next, and—ah—I said, "Would you be willing
to—let's be tentatively engaged with the understanding that, as
soon as we've seen each other, you can back out if you want
to?" She said yes, so we became engaged and we would talk

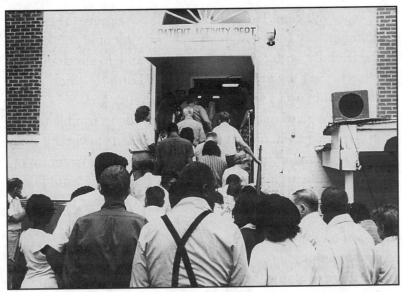

Patients line up to schedule their daily activities.

about our future. And she told me she had told so many people she was engaged to a fellow, and they would say, "Where's this phantom you're engaged with who never shows himself up?" And she kept after me to come see her in person. I didn't respond, and I was having a nice time talking with her on the phone. And with these other girls, too; and I was talking to these other girls. She told me if I didn't come to see her in person by a certain date, she was going to break off our engagement. But we still talked to each other for a while. Not long after that she got married.

I've talked to so many of those girls, and different girls. Some of them were grossly illiterate and some were grossly ignorant. I had a way of never being discourteous to any of them. And we have long known that conversation reveals character. Occasionally, a girl would call and I knew by her conversation she wasn't the lady she might have been. On some of these occasions my head would say, You better let this girl alone. But my heart would say, Remember the woman from Samaria who falls by the wayside well one day. There she came face to face with the Great Physician. He healed her ills, spoke peace to her heart, and on her way she went, rejoicing. And I would think that if I'll be friendly with this girl, I might be able to effect an introduction to the King of Kings and Lord of Lords, to whom all life is life eternal. And I would be friendly to this girl.

I know a great many zealots have gotten in trouble talking with girls on the phone, but I think one reason I never did get in trouble with any of them was that I had a way of never saying anything to them on the phone that a gentleman wouldn't be expected to say to a lady in person. And another reason was that I always played "lone wolf." I haven't seen it fail yet: get a bunch of boys together calling up girls, and some boy is going to say something off-color to some girl. Right there the trouble starts. I knew of one instance [when] a bunch of boys were together calling up girls, and one boy said something to a girl that was off-color and she just happened to repeat on the phone what he said. And her daddy happened to be where he could hear her side of the conversation, and for a long time that boy was having to dodge that girl's daddy. And I have had various experiences with these girls: I remember I was talking late with one girl one night and she felt like we had known each other a good while. Although we had never seen each other, she felt like she knew me well enough and had confidence in me to confide in me some of her little problems. I tried to help her as best I could. She seemed much relieved and much pleased with the solution I suggested. And when we said goodnight that night she said she would never love anybody else. But not long after that she married another man.

And maybe that's enough said about the girls.

QUESTION: Are there scheduled activities you have to take part in at Bryce, or do you have most of the free time you want?
ANSWER: We have mostly free time. I know on Saturdays and Sundays you can lie on your bed all day if you want. I don't want that; I'd rather get out and walk. A fellow pretty high up

in the hospital—he and I became acquainted with each other, and he asked me, little ol' me, "What about your recreational activities?" And he welcomed me to come by and visit him anytime I want to.

I told him about my recreational facilities—mostly of my own invention. I walk a great deal. My ward is about half a mile from the engineer's office. When I was working at the engineer's office, I'd walk from the ward to work in the morning and back to lunch. We eat in the dining room right next to my ward. Then I'd walk back to the engineer's office again, and then back in the evening, and that is approximately two miles. And I resolved to walk five miles everyday when I retired from the engineer's office, but I soon decided I didn't have to walk that much.

I reckon I usually walk about two miles a day and I take regular setting-up exercises. And I have special setting-up exercises that help to keep me from having asthma, and I like that one very much. A noted doctor came there to give physicals and he bragged on my breathing and said my breathing was excellent.

And so—maybe that's enough said on that question.

QUESTION: How old are you and how long have you been here?
ANSWER: I've been around there a quarter of a century and have been planning to write a book entitled *My Quarter Century Behind the Alabama Iron Curtain.* You asked about my age. I'm 73 going on 74, and hoping to have many more birthdays.

QUESTION: What were your duties at the engineer's office?
ANSWER: I remember one fellow asked me, "What do you do at the engineer's office?" I said, "Answering the phone, weighing trucks, and running errands." He said, "You mean sweeping floors?" "Yeah, that's part of it, too." He worked at what's called vegetable house, and he'd seen me sweeping floors.

QUESTION: Do you have any special philosophy of child raising—how to raise a child?

ANSWER: I know our parents didn't have to use much corporal punishment because they were intelligent enough to work us in a psychological way. Their law was our desire. Well, I think— I know there are children and there are children, just as there are adults and there are adults. I think you can work psychology on some of them, some of them are better with kindness, and some of them are just the opposite, just the other way. But I think it's best, it's better, if you can work psychology on them and cooperate with them. Act as though they were another grown person.

I watch "Hollywood Squares" regularly; I like those questions and answers. I believe it was the program where they asked, "When you go to your little boy's room, should you knock at his door before going in?" And I think that the parents should knock at the little boy's door before going in, and the answer was yes. They should respect his right the same as they would expect him to respect their rights.

Does anyone want to ask another question?

QUESTION: Where will you go if this legislation [passes]—where will you go if you have to leave Bryce? Do you have any relatives?

ANSWER: Yes, I have relatives, but they don't want me. I don't know how many years ago it was that the doctor asked me that, applying to my case. He says, "Well, we'll send you home if you want to go." I declined. I finally said that I know so well that they don't want me, and he left off urging me.

I found a pay station phone outside our dining room, and we go in about twelve o'clock in the day to eat lunch, then we come out about half past twelve. We go in the evening in the late afternoon about five and come out about half past five.

I tried to call one of my sisters long distance on one occasion, and the operator told me she had an unpublished phone. I didn't want to call her because I didn't know whether she'd want me to or not. I found the phone number of one of my other sisters, and I called her about the time of her birthday and wished her happy birthday. She told my other sister with the unpublished phone, and this other sister called me back on the following Monday night, and we've been calling and talking to each other ever since.

Somebody asked me what would I do if I get out of the hospital. Well, I was told a group of lawyers from Montgomery was going to come and talk to us—said they were coming one Wednesday—and they didn't come. They said they changed it to the following Monday, and they didn't come then and changed it to Tuesday, and didn't come then. But that Tuesday we were interviewed, and they asked me then what I would do.

I said, well, if they would put me out on the street—which I don't think they would—but if they were eager to discharge me or release me, I would say I've been saving. I've about $1,000 in my spending account. And I'll take out what I have in my spending account and go downtown and put it in the First National Bank and try to find me a room at the YMCA and, if they didn't have an opening, I'd ask them to recommend some nice place that had mostly women—I mean, mostly men. I'd have protection from the women; a man my age needs a certain amount of protection.

Anyway, there was a man who used to work at Bryce and he's retired now, and I think he owns a little horse farm on a little river—might be the Sipsey River. Anyway, when he was working there at the hospital, he and I talked this over. He knew he could get me out, he'd be willing to take me out to go live on his horse farm if I wanted to. And I've been thinking about that, and I would look into that if I was loose from the hospital, and I've thought of this and this was favorable with me. He might let me pay my board, at least part of my board, by doing chores on his farm such as feeding the livestock and all that.

But what I want eventually is to have a home way out, in

walking distance of the nearest village. I'd walk to the village everyday to get my groceries. I'd want to have a couple of dogs and a telephone. I could call my relatives. I found the pay station phone and called my sister and the other one called me, and we've been calling each other back and forth ever since. It's getting close enough to see; I don't know whether they'd want that or not. So, I declined from that.

QUESTION: I think the group would enjoy hearing some of your activities that have made money for you over the years at the hospital.

ANSWER: The time I came to Bryce Hospital, I didn't have enough money in the bank to employ a lawyer. I'm a resourceful fellow. I usually try to turn my disadvantage to my advantage. And when I'd get up with my work at the engineer's office, I'd walk out and watch for the Pepsi-Cola man, and when he'd arrive, I'd stand by his truck and say, "If your wife can't prepare meals, don't get a divorce. Keep her as a pet and serve Pepsi-Cola."

And he would say, "Here, have one." And after awhile, the RC Cola man would come. I'd advertise for him the same way and he'd say, "Here, have one." And the others would come. I'd advertise for them and sometimes the Frito Lay man would come and I'd help him in with his packages and he'd give me some of his wares. And the ice cream man would come and I'd help him in with his boxes.

Other patients would walk up to him and say, "Give me some," and he wouldn't give them any. I'd walk up to him and say, "Do you need me to help you in with your packages?" And as soon as we get his packages safely inside, I'd say, "Do you happen to have any mashed popsicles on board?" And he'd look around, and one day he found me a great big box full of mashed popsicles. I took them to the engineer's office, my place of employment, and passed them around.

And a few days later I found me another great big box full of mashed popsicles. I said I might as well cash in on these.

And I took them to the big kitchen and sold them to the people working in there for a nickel apiece. Now one man asked me, "How come we have to go to the canteen to get these and they charge six cents, and you bring them up here to us and don't charge but a nickel?" I'd say, "Well, these didn't come from town."

They would let the patients swap items of equal value in the canteen, and those bottles of carbonated water were too heavy for me to carry in my pocket, so I'd take them to the canteen and swap them for equal value in chewing gun, and then swap it over the counter for whatever I wanted. I'd save enough money to get a lawyer to get me out—reason I engaged in those activities.

And I know I didn't like any of the carbonated water men to see me advertising in front of the other, and one day they had a RC Cola truck, I think it was, and a Pepsi-Cola truck here at the same time, and I was just standing around waiting for one of them to pull off so I could start advertising for the other one. The Pepsi-Cola man said, "I don't see you advertising. What's the matter with you?" I said, "Well, some of my best advertising is behind-the-scene advertising. I go around and convince people they'd rather have Pepsi-Cola than something else." And he said, "Here, have one." I think that that day he gave me an armful.

I would save up my money and on the ward the patients would get boxes from home all the time. And this would be a typical example of what would happen: a patient would have, maybe, a can of pineapple in his box from home marked 25¢. But, because he didn't like pineapple, he'd sell that to somebody for a nickel cash.

This other fellow would turn around and sell me that same can of pineapple for a nickel cash. And I'd have it with me and I'd walk into the plumbing shop or electric shop or somewhere, and someone would say, "Go up there to the canteen and bring me five Coca-Colas." And I'd put that cash, cash quarter, in my pocket and spend tickets out of my canteen book for the Coca-

Colas. And I'd be making 400 percent profit and turning my tickets back into money all in one transaction.

And sometimes my sister would come to see me; she'd say, "How much do you have in your spending account?" I'd say, "I have plenty." And she'd say, "How much?" I'd say, "You don't need to put any in there."

On another occasion, during a question and answer session, Tom Hubbard was asked, "What would you do if you were released from Bryce?" He paused a very long time before answering: "I guess if you turned all of us out, a lot of us would come back, and I'd probably lead the way, 'cause I've been here so long I'd find it difficult to adjust outside."

About ten years after I retired, I had a phone call from Tom's sister who lived in northern Alabama, telling me that he was seriously ill and asking me to visit him at Bryce. I went to see Tom, who was jaundiced. Although flat on his back, he was right talkative. We visited together and I prayed with him. Only a few days later, his sister called again to tell me that Tom had died and had requested that I preach his funeral. Adolph Blakeney and I travelled in the hearse to the cemetery in Tom's hometown, where I conducted a graveside service. At his death Tom was in his late seventies.

-18-

How old the Golden Rule is, nobody knows. But on strangely graven stones and dateless parchments, students have traced the gist of it again and again. Judaism taught this basic truth, and Jesus re-phrased it: "Therefore all things whatsoever you would that men should do to you, do ye even so to them."* Simply stated, it means that I should treat others as I would be treated. Love my neighbor as myself; if I really do, I will be kind to him.

I believe that any creed, Christian or non-Christian, can accept the Golden Rule. It is the greatest of all ethical standards. It means that I must work unselfishly to obtain for others the very things I want for myself—and do this for them first. It is the foundation for good relations, and should be used in dealing with the mentally ill.

The opposite of the Golden Rule is putting one's own self-interests ahead of everything else. This attitude thinks only of a person's own needs and ignores the needs of his fellowmen. It takes no account of the human suffering it may cause. But in

---

* Matthew 7:12, King James Version

harming another, I really injure myself. The good I do to others is my own good; the harm I do another is my own harm.

Apparently the Golden Rule was seldom, if ever, used in the past in dealing with the mentally ill, or else these people would never have been taunted and teased, mimicked and mocked, flogged, thrown into dungeons and burned; nor would they have been neglected and forgotten by their relatives, the church, community, and state. Let us remember the Golden Rule in our treatment of them, realizing that anyone might find himself or herself in the same situation. *Do unto the mentally ill as if tomorrow you will be in their place.*

Maybe you think mental illness could not come to you or yours. People feel they are not in the slightest danger of being committed to a mental hospital, nor are their loved ones. But the fingers of circumstance reach out and often pick the choice one in the family. It does not respect class, color, creed, occupation, or social standing. It reaches the upper, middle, and lower classes. As its toll, it takes housewives, ministers, teachers, plumbers, social workers, textile workers, farmers, doctors, and lawyers.

It is possible that you may have to go to a mental hospital and remain there for the rest of your life. Many of these patients were pleasantly situated at your age. Their futures looked very bright. Suddenly it happened and they had to be confined. Ask yourself what you would have done if you had been in his or her place. Are you sure you would have done any better than they did?

Put yourself in their place for a day or a week, deprived of your job, separated from loved ones, feeling that you are stuck in an institution for life. If such a thing is remotely conceivable, see yourself forlorn, forsaken, forgotten by family, friends, and community. Ask yourself, "What would I be like if I were in their place? How would I want to be treated?" We all know how painful it is to be misunderstood, called mean names, snubbed, pushed to one side and dismissed. We also know the pleasure of a kind look, a warm greeting, a hand held out to help in distress. By that pain and by that pleasure let us be guided in what we should do for the mentally ill.

People have thought the mentally ill have no feelings, so they could be treated in almost any way—abused, beaten up, neglected, put in a hospital and forgotten—but, in reality, they are pleased and hurt just as others are. Often they are more sensitive, more easily hurt; that is one reason they are in a mental hospital.

Their bodies and minds may ache with a feeling of homesickness sometimes too deep for tears. Their souls often are bearing heavy burdens of guilt feelings, fear and insecurity, frustrations of love; feelings of disgrace, hurt, pride, despair, helplessness, hopelessness; loss of faith in God, loved ones, and themselves.

We also find those who long for deep breaths of the Spirit of the living God to give them new life and strength. Often their hearts are broken and need binding up; their souls are battered and need to be soothed with the peace of God.

The Golden Rule says, in effect: Turn the situation around. Put yourself in the other fellow's place. If you have a relative, friend, neighbor or patient who is mentally ill, put yourself in his or her place and treat them as you would like to be treated. This applies to doctors who speak harshly to heavyhearted families who come for a word of encouragement. It also applies to attendants who push old folks along too fast, or rush them by cramming food down their throats before they have time to chew it thoroughly, or otherwise treat them roughly. It also applies to relatives who visit them and, just to get away, say, "We'll be back in a few minutes after we talk to the doctor"—and never come back.

There are some families who put those they have loved in a mental hospital and then ignore them. They never write or go to see them, never send them any spending money, never bring them home on a visit. I have heard of some relatives of patients who have visited in the city where the hospital is located, and even passed by the hospital, but never stopped to visit their family members. Perhaps their relatives are afraid to have any contact with the mentally ill, lest it work against their personal, social, or professional interests.

If we would help the mentally sick, the best place to begin is with ourselves. Every change for their betterment should begin in our minds and hearts. Until one can see good in the mentally ill, he or she cannot work very effectively with them. Let us never hold them in contempt, never humiliate even the humblest, never withhold from any the opportunity to be and do the best of which he or she is capable. Seek to assure each one of our respect, our confidence, and our good will, knowing that only thus can we expect to be really helpful to them. When in doubt what to do for them, do the loving thing.

Mentally sick people respond to kindness, love, and understanding just as other people do. They need encouragement. People should never talk in their presence about their not having any sense, or let them think their case is hopeless. They respond to the faith we have in them. We should, however, be careful not to build up any false hopes in them. Let them know we still believe in them and that they are still important to God.

Some people seem to think it does not matter what is told to the mentally ill. But if we lie to them, they feel they have been double-crossed and let down. They lose confidence in their family or others. They say, "How can I trust my people anymore? I've been lied to so many times." They should be told the truth about going to a mental hospital.

The mentally sick need to be treated with kindness and intelligence and to be guided with firm but loving wisdom at all times. It has often been otherwise in the past: when they were spoken to or given orders, they should have been spoken to kindly, softly, never harshly; then they would have responded more readily, just as you and I would.

They wanted to know the reason for an act, just as you or I

would. I believe the informed person is the most cooperative person, but the medical profession as a whole in the past thought it unwise to inform the mentally ill. Or the doctors probably thought it quite impossible to explain things in the short time they had with the patients.

But the mentally ill told me they did not like to be pushed around. They wanted to know why they were moved from ward to ward. They felt they were due this respect.

I believe the patients would have cooperated better if informed. But without an explanation, they became more insecure, which might have led to failure in their making a comeback.

Those who have responsibilities in a mental hospital should always remember that a mental hospital is not a compromise between a general hospital and a prison, but it is a therapeutic community. The aim and purpose of psychiatric treatment, as I understand it, is to liberate the mentally ill from the restrictions and suffering occasioned by mental illness.

Patients often have the capacity for a considerable degree of responsibility and initiative. We should assume that they are trustworthy until their behavior proves the opposite to be true. In a well-run mental hospital, only a small minority of the mentally ill need to be in locked wards. Disturbing behavior is not to be ignored, but good behavior should be encouraged and antisocial behavior met by appropriate measures.

When a patient is disturbing others and is moved to another ward, he should be told why, and that the move is not a punishment. At the earliest opportunity he should be returned to his former ward. Insofar as is possible, when performing their duties, psychiatrists should seek the cooperation of the mentally ill.

Every means possible should be used to preserve their dignity, self-respect, and sense of individuality. When one is deprived of personal possessions and clothes, thrown into a strange place and locked up, it comes as a severe blow which is hard to overcome.

THROUGH THESE EYES

Worship services are now conducted regularly in the hospital's Bryant-Jordan Chapel, named for famed football coaches Paul "Bear" Bryant of Alabama and Ralph "Shug" Jordan of Auburn.

Sometimes attendants, who have a wonderful opportunity to help, do not seem to realize it. There is the case of an attendant who said to a quiet, elderly man on the ward, "Get out of my way, or I'll knock the hell out of you." Judging by their behavior, some attendants appear to be sicker in mind than some of those in their care. But there is also an attendant who worked several years on a disturbed ward and who told me, "I treat my men with the same consideration I would treat my father if he were on this ward."

I know of one woman who, after her release from a mental hospital, told some friends, "No matter what you say, it sounds crazy. You might be as serious as anyone on the outside, but when you're in such an institution you are considered crazy, so whatever you say is crazy. You might have a pain and tell someone about it, but it sounds crazy because it is from a supposedly crazy person. That starts you on the road to that helpless feeling and the feeling that you have no friends."

She continued, "When a lot of people arrive at a mental hospital, they are just nervous, as I was. But nervous or crazy, you are treated as a child and a crazy person. I resented the way they talked to me, and I resented the way they ordered me around. Resentment brings punishment. This goes on and on until you are confused, and finally just kind of give up because you begin to believe you really are crazy."

Many wait in the hospital for weeks, months, and even years for the forces of nature to renew their health and strength. This waiting is not easy. There is impatience and worry and a desire to get out of the hospital and back to home, work, and the normal activities of life. There is apprehension and fearful uncertainty as to how they will be received by family, friends, church and community when they return to the outside world; the very thought of contending with the outside world frightens them.

The fear of life brought some people to the hospital. They just could not take it; they could not cope with life and have come to the hospital for refuge. They feel more secure in the hospital than in an insecure world outside; they are happier there than outside in a hostile environment such as they have known in the past, and fear they will have to go back to it. They feel the world outside will not welcome them, and that they will have to face pointing fingers and the scorn of a society that does not understand them.

When the mentally ill are improved or cured, they often go back to homes where there are hostilities. These hostilities contributed to their having to go to the hospital in the first place. Relatives can cause much distress by their negative attitudes, and remarks such as "You are still crazy; if you don't behave, we're going to send you back to the hospital." One young lady told me she got jittery under such treatment and said, "Just take me back to the hospital. I'd rather be there where they are kind and understand me."

Many others told me of similar thoughts: they would rather be at the hospital than at home. They explained that they are

THROUGH THESE EYES

treated better there than at home. One patient, David Wilson, was about 35 years of age. He was valuable help on his ward and attended church services and recreational programs. He had been in the hospital five years. He said, "I'd rather be here than go back home, it being what it is. If I go back, there might be trouble."

Mary Morrison came to the hospital highly nervous and fearful. While there she sang in the choir and made many friends on the wards. As soon as she was able, she went home to her people. After a short stay, she returned to the hospital. I asked her why she came back. "Because you people here are kind, loving, and understanding. If my people had been, I could have stayed home with them where I belong. I wanted to stay but just couldn't, the way they treated me."

The mentally sick are never helped by faultfinding or criticism, hate or shame, by saying nasty words about them. Harsh words, critical or hurtful words, contentious and bitter words never help them, but only confuse, upset, and depress them. Sometimes members of a family are so cantankerous, cruel, unkind, unloving, and without understanding as to make it impossible for one to have a sound mind. So we see there is great need somehow to teach the family how to treat the mentally ill when they have recovered and return home. Often when they go home on a visit, relatives and others look at them with fear-filled eyes. Everything on the outside makes them worse. In the hospital there is refuge of a sort.

Some patients cannot long endure the confusion of freedom outside, the burden of real life, and so are glad to return to the hospital as a place where nothing is required of them, where they have no responsibility. Why should they try to leave it?

When the mentally ill have recovered and return to their churches and communities, about all they want is cordiality. Many Christians have been almost completely without the spiritual gentleness and love which the mentally ill need so much. They have condemned them and assumed a holier-than-thou attitude and dismissed it at that. We should be tolerant of the imperfections of these brothers and sisters, as we would wish them to be tolerant of us in the same situation.

Ophelia Brown returned home, but after four months was back at the hospital. When asked why, she replied, "I was well enough to face the world but the world was not well enough to face me."

Then she related an experience at church. Two women sitting nearby, whom she did not know, looked her squarely in the face. "That common woman," one remarked. The whispers and glances were more than she could take.

Ministers, especially, can set an example for others. If the public sees the minister is cordial and reasonably helpful, others will often follow his or her example in their treatment of mental patients who have returned home.

It is taken for granted that the church interest itself with the ministration of comfort and consolation while its members are hospitalized, but it has even greater responsibility to them when they return to society again. It should see that they are accepted, respected, encouraged, and given a fair chance to make good.

A young man in his twenties went to Bryce for several months. Soon after his arrival there, a member of his church wrote, "When Bill comes home, there will be many fine Christians to help in any way they can to encourage, instruct, and help him." I passed these words on to Bill, and they helped to keep his spirits high until he could be released.

These people yearn to be accepted when they return to their communities. They want others to believe they are doing the best they can, even though they may fail. It may be they had left undone things which they ought to have done, and done those things which they ought not to have done. If so, they plead for your patience and understanding, for many of them have made mistakes not intentionally, but through ignorance or sickness of the mind.

Louise had been twice in the hospital. In speaking to me

about going home she said, "We do not want to be pitied or petted or have baby-fied sympathy. If you want to call it sympathy, call it understanding sympathy. We do want to be able to feel we are still a part of society and accepted as soon as we are able to go out and mix or find our place with people again."

Arletha Rogers had been a social worker before her commitment to the hospital. After several months there, she returned to her home and community. Soon she was back at the hospital. When asked why, she remarked, "Prison bars are not as bad as social bars."

In everyday life Ruth Stubblefield worked in a novelty shop. She had come to the hospital for the seventh time, her mind overly stimulated. After six months she returned home. She wrote to me: "Homecoming was a happy event. Each time, I am held in awe at the many friends who are as happy to have me home as I am to be home. And though I am hurt a wee bit inside at having failed them, their faith in me is what always renews my courage and determination to try again. And when I add to the friends who welcome me home, you friends who send me home—my cup runneth over."

Trouble comes to every family. None of us is safe from calamity. It can be cancer, it can be broken relationships, it can be poverty. Mental illness is no different from these. There is no shame in cancer. There is no shame in poverty. And there is no shame in mental illness. Those so afflicted are not to be hidden from the outside world as if they were "living sorrows" to their families. Our parents, our children, and our friends need our love and support when trouble is visited upon them: through us God can ease their way.

Let us think of these dear ones not as they were when they had to go to a hospital, but as they can be when we treat them as human beings, as brothers and sisters. Let us treat them as we would want to be treated if the same misfortune would befall us. If everyone who associates with the mentally ill lived up to his or her highest understanding of the Golden Rule, allowing the light of God's love to dispel ignorance and fear, a great and wonderful transformation would be brought about in our mental hospitals, families, churches, and communities.

I have a part to play and so do you: we are our brothers' and sisters' keepers.

EPILOGUE

My ministry at Bryce lasted 14 years. It was the happiest ministry I ever had and I left it reluctantly—unwillingly—in early 1965. I was 66 years old, a year older than the mandatory retirement age, and I was told that I must leave. I found my work so immensely satisfying that I had never given a thought to retiring.

I was deeply attached to the patients and thought carefully about how to announce my departure, choosing to do so at a Sunday morning worship service. I used as my text words of God to the children of Israel: "I have loved you with an everlasting love."* I reminded my congregation that this was just as true for us today, and spoke about the fact, the nature, and the eternity of God's love. I then made my painful announcement and told them that parting would be difficult for me, but that thoughts of them would remain with me in the years ahead. I asked God's blessing on these friends for all the days of their lives.

That was 30 years ago, and although I found myself with little to do in the first six months of retirement, life had a way of

---

* Jeremiah 31:3, Revised Standard Version

calling for my service after that. An elder from a Presbyterian church visited me and asked if I would be their pastor for a few weeks until the congregation could find a minister. I turned him down, but he returned a few days later with another elder, renewing the request. This time I agreed to serve them, and the "few weeks" stretched into five and a half years. One of my congregation was asked by an outsider if the Methodist minister "preached Presbyterian sermons," and was told that most of them would pass very well for Presbyterian.

Then I served concurrently two Methodist churches, Hannah and Sand Springs in Pickens County, for six years, and I have fond memories of those congregations. Following this I served as associate minister at St. Mark Church in Northport for almost a year and then ministered to the good people at Union Chapel for a year. At the request of my district superintendent, I went to Andrews Chapel for a very satisfying ministry lasting five years. These latter churches are in Tuscaloosa County.

During our more than 50 years as husband and wife, Clytie Mae and I had returned annually to her home in east Texas, often for family reunions. On one of those occasions in the early 1980's, I arose at the end of a reunion banquet and stated that, after finishing Southern Methodist University in Dallas and marrying Clytie Mae, had I known all those long trips would follow, I'd have just stayed in the Texas Conference! Certainly that would have been agreeable to my wife.

As I spoke, little did I realize that this would be the last of those long, but very important, trips to visit Clytie Mae's family. After most of the crowd had left, two of my wife's sisters drew me to one side and asked me what was the matter with Clytie Mae. I didn't understand what they meant, and they assured me that she was much changed from the year before.

When we returned home to Alabama, I consulted our doctor and was told that Clytie Mae had Alzheimer's disease. Memories of events that I had ignored at the time—as being of no permanent consequence—crowded my thoughts: Clytie

Mae's twice telling me of narrow escapes from driving accidents; her struggling to express thoughts that slipped from her mind as she spoke, then asking me, "Am I crazy? Am I losing my mind? Will I have to go to Bryce Hospital?"

Even as her condition deteriorated, my own health took a turn that was as disruptive as it was unexpected: my eyesight began to fail steadily and I learned that I had macular degeneration. I began having to stop other customers when I went grocery shopping to ask them to read the labels and prices of items I wanted to buy. I soon discontinued our subscription to the daily newspaper, a paper I could no longer read. Nor did I any longer have use for a telephone directory. Driving my car became impossible. I was unable to take care of Clytie Mae and myself.

I sold our Northport home with the flower and vegetable garden that had been my pleasure for 25 years, hastily disposed of our two cars and most of my library and our furnishings and personal belongings, then moved with Clytie Mae to Skyland Oaks Retirement Center in adjacent Tuscaloosa. Only three months later I had to transfer Clytie Mae to a nursing home.

With my vision gone, home gone, beloved wife gone, newspapers and cherished books gone, I went through great stress. During this period Carol Rhodes, a friend to us and secretary for St. Mark United Methodist Church where we worshipped, called and asked if I would like for some persons from the church to come and read for me. She recruited several ladies as readers, and two men who took turns driving me weekly to visit Clytie Mae and attend to errands and personal business.

For my part, I made a conscious, deliberate attempt to build a *new* life for myself. My health was excellent, apart from my eyesight. Although I could not recognize faces, I had some peripheral vision and could get around quite well with that. I was serving as chaplain at Skyland Oaks and preached there every Sunday. During all my years in the pulpit I had used and depended on sermon notes; now I no longer could read them. I

Chaplain Thomas, seated at right, returned to Bryce in 1976 to help observe the United States' bicentennial.

would have to learn to memorize my sermons—and I did. I reminded myself every morning that "something good is going to happen to me today." If it had not happened by two o'clock, I went looking for it.

My readers—Marian Hawkins, Kay Culton, Virginia Caine, Sherry Fisher Singley, Annette Walker, Martha McDee, Annie Laura Leonard, and John Mitchell—read books and discussed ideas with me, attended to my mail, wrote correspondence, and wrote checks for me. Barbara Jordan from the Tuscaloosa Public Library provided me with many audio tapes and records, taking a personal interest in discovering what I would enjoy and becoming my friend. Members of St. Mark—first Bill and Beth Yessick, later, an entire Sunday school class—"adopted" me, taking turns coming for me and driving me to church there each Sunday after I had preached my early morning sermon at Skyland Oaks.

I made many new friends, and old friendships became richer. I found time for deep reflection, time which often had been lacking in the past. I picked up the pages of this manuscript once more and brought my book to its present fruition. I frequently preached at churches as guest minister. I even played the part of a rambunctious small boy in a play at Skyland Oaks, wearing short pants and a wig and hopping around doing a jig! No longer necessary is the deliberate effort to build a new life; that life is simply here, present and satisfying with each new day.

My wife departed this earthly life January 19, 1993. For six years Jimmie Mills and Abe VanderMeer had remained faithful in driving me to visit Clytie Mae, often joining me as I sang hymns or prayed at her bedside, sharing my loss of her, even in her presence. For their kindness I will be ever grateful, and now Clytie Mae is able to know the same appreciation.

When death claimed her physical presence, I thought back to the time many years before when Clytie Mae had travelled to India for a month's visit. As I watched her enter the plane I thought, "She's going to be gone for a long time and I will miss her very much. But *we will meet again!*" In some ways she had left me many years before her passing, but now I am aware of her here with me, and someday our reunion will be complete. We will meet again.

Throughout these retirement years—decades of unexpected change and adjustment, deep satisfactions and frustrations, wrenching loss and gracious renewal—my thoughts have never been far from those I promised to remember, the patients at Bryce. Of all my professional identities, the one that comes first always to my mind is that of myself as "Bryce Hospital's first chaplain." The patients there—my charges, sometimes my friends—rewarded my ministry to them with such responses as they were able to give: occasionally scornful, frequently loving, usually candid, but always giving me a sense that I was exactly where God wanted me to be.

After my retirement I sometimes received a phone call or letter from a former resident at the hospital. Each one said, "I just want to thank you for what you meant to me while I was at

Bryce Hospital. Without you, I never would have made it."

One patient in particular—Millie Walters—returned to her home and has been a faithful friend all these many years, sending me Christmas cards and notes, inquiring about my wife, occasionally telephoning and bringing me news of others we had both known at Bryce. I find such expressions both sufficient and ample reward for my labors.

I wish I could answer your curiosity and concern, as well as my own, about the whereabouts or ends of all those patients to whom I've introduced you. The fact is that, unless a former patient contacted me, I usually did not know what had become of him or her. Edith Collin, removed so suddenly and frighteningly from her home by sheriff's deputies as she prepared her family's breakfast, made a good adjustment to the hospital and then began helping me with my secretarial work. She was an excellent typist, and I was sorry to lose her, but very glad when she was eventually released from Bryce.

The fate of the other patients is best understood through the wisdom of the Reverend Paul Blackmon.

Brother Blackmon was a patient at Bryce when I arrived and was still there when I left. He was always immaculately dressed, sang solos during worship in a beautiful tenor voice, and regularly helped out in the Recreation Department. He was a real prince of a fellow and I loved him dearly. He visited me often in my office, and on one occasion asked, "How far would one have to go to go beyond the love of God?"

"You tell me," I replied. "I would like *your* answer."

He stood up straight, pointed his outstretched arms east and west, and said, "If you go on and on either way, you can never go beyond the love of God." I agreed. Then he turned his arms north and south and made the same statement. I agreed again. Then, with one arm pointing heavenward and the other downward, he said, "It doesn't matter how far one goes; no one can go beyond the love of God, no matter which direction he takes."

None of them has gone—or ever will go—beyond the love of God.

THROUGH THESE EYES

ACKNOWLEDGMENTS

During my years as chaplain at Bryce Hospital in Tuscaloosa, Alabama, I wrote many brief notes of happenings there, without any special intention of writing a book. Later, that idea began to take shape in my mind. After retiring I completed the manuscript—or rather, thought that I did—and a Birmingham friend, JOELLYNN HEATON, transcribed it on a word processor for me, giving the book its initial structure. However, early in the 1980's my eyesight deteriorated rapidly and I kind of gave up the idea of publishing it.

In 1986 my wife, Clytie Mae, and I moved to Skyland Oaks Retirement Center in Tuscaloosa, but soon thereafter she had to go to a nursing home because of advancing Alzheimer's disease. About that time, CAROL BAILEY RHODES, secretary at St. Mark United Methodist Church in nearby Northport where we worshipped, phoned and asked if I would like for some persons from the church to come and read to me. Carol recruited six ladies from St. Mark and another church as readers. According to their schedules, some came once a week, others every other week or once a month. Two men alternated in taking me weekly to visit my wife and do necessary errands.

I told ANNETTE F. WALKER, one of my readers, about the manuscript. She read part of it and urged me to bring it out of the closet and publish it. VIRGINIA BRINSON CAINE, another reader, began regular work on the manuscript with me; we examined it critically and altered it accordingly. During this process DR. KATHERINE ALEXANDER, director of life writing and historical preservation at Shelton State Community College, also in Tuscaloosa, read the text and made the highly constructive suggestion that the book be in the first person, rather than the third person as I had written it. Virginia suggested that her friend JEAN MARIE ARMISTEAD read the book and make suggestions. Jean brought an entirely new perspective and once again the book was dissected and examined critically, this time by the three of us. Jean made suggestions about additional background and changes in structure.

Throughout the entire editing process I was deeply concerned about three chapters which were missing. I knew I had written this additional material, but several searches had failed to turn it up and I knew I could not reconstruct the text from memory. We went ahead without it.

We consulted HARVEY FRETWELL, director of community relations at Bryce Hospital and a longtime friend, who gave us invaluable information about shock treatment, commitment procedures, and those federal court cases which produced far-reaching changes in mental health services statewide, and at Bryce Hospital in particular.

DR. ADOLPH L. BLAKENEY, associate chaplain and, later, director of staff training at Bryce, gave me a copy of a tape recording of talks made by longtime Bryce patient Tom Hubbard (not his real name). The material from the tape is incorporated into a chapter of this book.

Finally, just as the book seemed to have taken its final form, the three missing chapters turned up—all six of them! CAROL BAILEY RHODES, who had already processed one major revision, didn't waver a bit when told that there was still another revision and several additional chapters to be typed.

My son ALAN "AL" ROLAND THOMAS, my daughter-in-law GYPSY SKELTON THOMAS, and my grandson PAUL THOMAS then read the manuscript, and Al contributed his talent and experience to a third and final revision.

LARRY THOMAS, another one of my sons, used his photographic abilities in producing the cover pictures and some of the pictures inside the book. KATHLEEN V. FETTERS, medical librarian at Bryce Hospital, helped select other pictures from the hospital's archives to further illustrate the book. DR. THOMAS SIDNEY TARWATER furnished a photograph of his father, the late Dr. James Sidney "Sid" Tarwater, the hospital administrator during my tenure there.

I am very grateful to each of these wonderful people, for without their help, this book would not have been written.

O the Daniel Thomas